John C. McLoughlin, a zoologist and bio-
scientific illustrator, has spent much of his
life in New York City, although he now
divides his time between New Mexico and
the Eastern Seaboard. He is the founder of
the New Mexico Zoological Survey and is
currently at work on a book about
dinosaurs.

THE ANIMALS AMONG US

John C. McLoughlin

THE
ANIMALS
AMONG
US
Wildlife
in the City

The Viking Press • New York

Copyright © J. C. McLoughlin, 1978

First published in 1978 by The Viking Press
625 Madison Avenue, New York, N.Y. 10022

Published simultaneously in Canada by
Penguin Books Canada Limited

LIBRARY OF CONGRESS CATALOGING IN PUBLICATION DATA
McLoughlin, John C
The animals among us.
Includes index.
1. Urban fauna.   I. Title.
QH541.5.C6M3   591.9'173'2   78–6642
ISBN 0–670–12759–0

Printed in the United States of America
Set in Linotype Times Roman

This book is dedicated to
Carole and Ariana

Contents

Preface   ix

Introduction   1

1   The House Sparrow   21

2   The Starling   55

3   The Pigeon   75

4   The Mouse   103

5   Rats   123

6   The Lesser Tenants   149

7   Almost Inquilines   177

Index   189

vii

Preface

O nce upon a time I rented a fancy house from a rich lawyer. In one of the rooms of the house was a large off-yellow shag rug. I have long been of the opinion that the Devil invented shag rugs, and I undertook to remove the hairy monster without delay. In so doing I noticed a little animal running among the fibers of the rug and, being what I am (a zoologist), I paused to catch it, to see what manner of life might be living off the labors of this lawyer. While catching the animal, a tiny beetle of the family Staphylinidae, I noticed the movements of other creatures and in a short time had collected from the rug a series of animals representing three classes, seven families, and twelve genera of the majestic phylum Arthropoda.

Now, a limited environment such as this shag rug (about 9 square meters in area) must have some fairly intense energy input to support such a varied population of animals. Since it was in the house, the rug contained no green plants to trap energy for the use of its resident organisms, so I had to search for other sources. The rug lay on the floor of a room in which people had been accustomed to eat while watching the television. The process of carrying food from kitchen to television had been inefficient enough over the years to permit a buildup of organic matter at the base of the hairy fibers of the rug, organic matter consisting mainly of spilled snackies that never responded to the ministrations of broom or vacuum cleaner. The small scavengers were supported by this lucrative ecological niche and supported in their own turn a tiny population of predators—spiders and pseudoscorpions—who stalked the woolly forest like tigers in the night. Beneath the feet of the attorney owning this house existed a fantastic underworld of animal life whose shelter was provided by the shag and whose energy was derived almost entirely from by-products of the cultural symbiosis between consumer and television set.

If one shag rug can support such a diversity of animal life, consider a whole building, or a nation, or the world industrial culture! In short, from a nasty old shag rug was born this little book. In it I have made an attempt to understand some of the exquisite adaptations made by animal life to the many unique microhabitats created by the activity of human beings. In allowing the animals themselves to do the teaching, I have been led along some strange paths in time and space. Always, however, I have returned to the realization that the living system is a thing of unspeakable toughness and resilience, and of endless beauty—even when other members of the system are competing with us tooth and nail for our food and space. It is my hope that some of this beauty shows through in the natural histories to follow, that our inquilines, partners with us in the ancient, stately dance of life, may offer us a new viewpoint from which to admire the gorgeous ballroom that is Earth.

Introduction

We have become an elemental. In the brief ten thousand years since the inception of agriculture, humans have changed the face of the earth to such an extent as to have rendered it an artifact, a creature of man. The ancient and conservative forces of organic evolution have given way to the giddy passing of technological information between individuals and generations, made possible by that uniquely human specialization, true language.

The gigantic human brain has enabled its possessors to conceive of themselves in a fashion new to the world. Seeing the effects of their ingenuity on their environment, early agricultural humans felt somehow separate from the rest of the living system and constructed elaborate mythologies to support this point of view. The earth was created for the use of Man, they said. All entities became subject to the whim of Man, and to the whim of the gods that Man created and that served His purposes.

The appearance of the first towns furthered this outlook with their increased impact on the landscape around them. Forests fell before the ax, wild plains were set to the plow, and cities with highly organized legal and religious systems evolved in the twinkling of an eye. Deviation from culturally established behavioral norms was meticulously punished, and the myth of human supranaturalness was petrified in tradition and law.

It was little more than a hundred years ago that civilized humanity first began to pass beyond this sort of thinking. With the origination of Darwinian evolutionary theory, we began again to see ourselves as part of the whole of life. More recent discoveries in the fields of biology, the behavioral sciences, and chemistry show us that earthly life is a single family united by the molecular ribbons from which all living matter crystallizes.

From our fellow beings we are beginning to learn more about ourselves. The fierce beauty of the human experience is slowly becoming explicable in the light of the behavior and construction of our less brilliant relatives throughout the living system. With an unprejudiced eye we may see our own history paraphrased in the countless nonhuman lives around us, even as our cleverness continues to decimate those lives.

There are some animals, though, that have profited from the rise of civilized humanity. Through a fortuitous combination of behavioral adaptability and rapidity of generation, they have become an integral part of the human cultural experience. It is where human activity is most intense, in the great urban-industrial complexes of the twentieth century, that such animals abound. Sharing human food and habitat, migrations, diseases, history, they remain wild while bound to us in their dependence on the fruits of technology.

These are the inquilines of humanity. Hated and despised for their competition with us, feared and admired for their persistence and vitality, trapped and poisoned through thousands of years, they continue to participate in our lives—with enthusiasm. They have made our cities their habitat in a world impoverished of wildernesses. They can be the most accessible source of some sense of wildness to millions of people, and uniquely so.

Their wilderness is us.

Inquilinism is a form of symbiosis, of "living together." All organisms on this planet are symbiotes one with another, each a part of the thin and incredibly elastic membrane we call the living system. In a more specific sense, however, the word "symbiosis" refers to relationships between different species whose interaction is extended and to some degree intimate. Several different kinds of symbioses are recognized, based on the extent and sort of dependencies exhibited in the association, and to understand something of their nature we must examine some of the history of life itself.

The earliest earthly life of which we are now aware lived some three billion years ago. Although these forms are fragmentary and poorly pre-

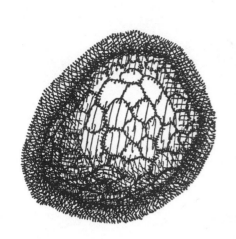

Impressions of early plants preserved in the Gunflint Chert of Ontario. These microscopic forms, here magnified 1500 times, closely resemble bacteria and blue-green algae of the present. The wide variety of forms represented in the deposit suggests a long history of life on earth prior to the fossilization of these specimens.

served, they resemble relatively intact fossils from such deposits as Canada's two-billion-year-old Gunflint Chert and represent a fairly late state in the evolution of life. These forms appear to have been blue-green algae, the simplest known living things capable of photosynthesizing carbohydrates from carbon dioxide and water with the energy of the sun.

The process of photosynthesis releases molecular oxygen, a chemical so corrosive that it eats away metal and rock. In the early seas and atmosphere there was very little free oxygen, and living forms survived without it in an ancient and successful metabolic mode called anaerobism. The success of photosynthesizers resulted in a gradual increase in the amount of oxygen in the environment, and oxygen was a deadly poison to anaerobes and early photosynthesizers. A new selective pressure came to bear on the young living system, which responded by inventing *animals*.

The animals are currently estimated to have first evolved some seven hundred million years ago, relative newcomers in the four-billion-year history of the living system. These creatures metabolized organic matter by using the very oxygen that poisoned most of their plant competitors at the start, in the process called respiration, which seems to have evolved from photosynthesis. Animals were to a certain extent motile; they were able to locate, move toward, and consume other living entities, the photosynthesizers from which they derived the matter and energy necessary to continue functioning.

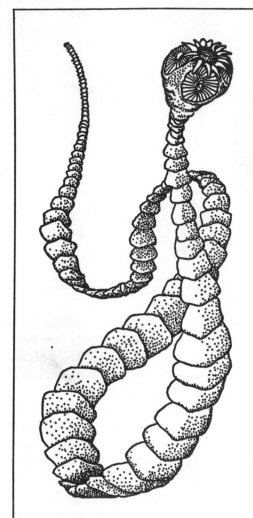

A tapeworm of the genus *Taenia,* parasitic in the intestines of vertebrates. The animal lives on food digested by its host; it is reduced to a set of hooks with which to attach to the wall of the host intestine, some suckers with which to absorb food, and a chain of independent reproductive systems, or proglottids, composing the bulk of the monster.

Photosynthesizers, which are able to construct molecules around bits of energy derived directly from the sun, are said to be autotrophs, or "'self-feeders." The rest of the living system, which must snatch its energy from autotrophs, is composed of heterotrophs, "other-feeders." Heterotrophs may be said to be parasitic on the world of green plants, stealing energy from autotrophs but permitting them to reproduce sufficiently to support themselves and their parasites. Parasitism, then, is a symbiosis in which one living form benefits at the expense of another, usually without killing the host. Parasites have evolved some improbable forms and ways in their use of fellow organisms. A characteristic of parasites is their usual loss of function and/or form in coevolving with their hosts—from the inability of the first animals to photosynthesize food to the loss by mistletoe of leaves and roots as it took up an existence parasitic on other plants. Many parasitic insects that spend their lives inside a living host have lost legs, wings, and eyes to become shapeless sacs of reproductive matter. Similar changes occur in worms and crustaceans that adopt a parasitic existence dependent on vertebrates. Birds such as cowbirds and cuckoos, which are brood parasites that lay their eggs in other birds' nests, have lost some of the complex social behavior based on brood-raising and are often entirely unable to build nests themselves.

Certain fungi were among the earliest parasites, living on green algae and utilizing the food photosynthesized by their hosts. The resulting fungus-alga symbiosis was ancestral to the lichens, which are actually two-way relationships beneficial to both partners. The fungus partner in a lichen uses food produced by its alga, which in turn enjoys protection by the fungus from desiccation and may utilize minerals made available by fungal metabolism of the substance to which the lichen is anchored. Such symbiosis to the benefit of all involved is called mutualism. The most familiar examples of mutualism are probably those between human beings and domesticated animals and plants. Such creatures as peanuts, pigs, and pear

Gray crustose lichen living on sandstone, magnified 40 times. Lichens are often the first plants to appear in places denuded of life: they are able to metabolize rock into the first inkling of soil necessary to support the growth of higher plants. Such a crustose lichen may grow only an inch a century in harsh environments, but the vitality of this fungus-alga mutualism suggests that lichens may be one of the few earthly forms capable of surviving the climate of Mars.

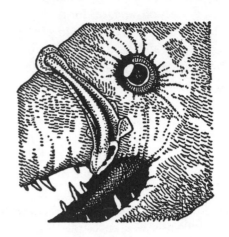

A brilliant blue-and-silver cleaner wrasse inspects the teeth of a willing moray eel. Unrelated fish performing similar services for predatory animals have paralleled the wrasse's coloring, and the sight of such small creatures slipping into (and out of!) the mouths of mighty predators is an inspiring example of mutualism.

trees are distributed on nearly every continent, living alongside the humans who tend them and utilize them. Among other animals, the evolution of mutualism is often accompanied by the adoption, in one partner, of behavioral, olfactory, or visual characteristics signaling the desirability of its presence for the well-being of another. Animals feeding on the external parasites of larger animals, subject as they may be to predation by their clients, often display conspicuous color patterns or ritualistic behavior to prevent unfortunate errors. These color patterns are common in fish such as the cleaner wrasse, whose specialty is removing parasites from larger animals, such as the moray eel (see illustration). So effective is the brilliant blue-and-silver striping of the wrasse in gaining it safe access to the parasites of large predators that a parasitic fish, the false cleaner, has evolved similar coloration, enabling it to approach and bite flesh from large fish expecting only a grooming session.

The advent of animals complicated the autotroph-heterotroph symbiosis immensely, causing the rapid evolution of new forms. Lacking the ability to photosynthesize, animals experienced selective pressure toward the invention of a bewildering array of methods to succeed in the competition for food. Secondary consumers—carnivores—evolved, and a new symbiosis, predation, was created. Animals have evolved complex predator-prey relationships in which their populations are nearly always closely associated. Such a close association occurs between certain deer and the wolves that prey on them; the deer feed the wolves, which in turn keep the deer population healthy by exerting pressure on the ill and unfit. Populations of deer kept in check by the ever-vigilant wolves are less of a burden on the plants that sustain them; the wolves in turn must maintain strength and guile to keep up with the healthy population of deer.

Another form of symbiosis is commensalism, "sharing the table," which involves organisms that associate for the benefit of one species, at little or no disadvantage to another. Such relationships are usually found

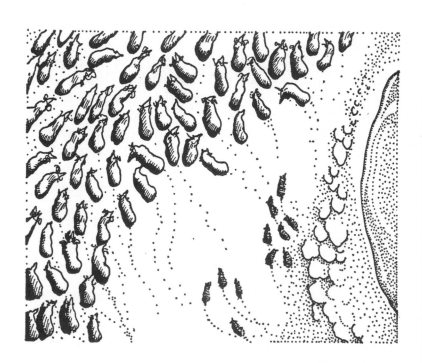

Aerial view of wolves traveling with a herd of caribou. When the wolves are satiated, the caribou show no fear of them. Signals passed among hungry wolves are understood by the caribou as reason to move quickly; weak animals are thus filtered out of the herd and converted into wolf. Caribou herds within the Arctic Circle supported predatory populations of both wolves and humans for thousands of years until the advent of firearms upset the balance among them and caused the decline of both wolves and caribou.

in association with a food source common to the species involved, hence the name. In Africa, certain antelope are commensal with ostriches; both forms feed in open land, and the antelope make use of the superior height and eyesight of ostriches in spotting potential danger. The ancestors of domestic dogs may originally have been commensals of human hunters, profiting from the superior strength and ingenuity of the latter in killing the animals on whose remains they scavenged. This relationship ultimately evolved into a form of mutualism whose product, of course, is Man's Best Friend.

Inquilinism is a symbiosis sharing certain qualities of both parasitism and commensalism. It occurs in nearly every place where life has evolved the potential for building. Derived from the Latin *inquilinus*, "tenant," the word refers to a relationship in which one species builds a nest and another moves into that nest without displacing the builder. Building, an activity shared by relatively few animals, is in essence an alteration of the environment to create a new habitat suitable to the requirements of the builder. Such a new habitat may be suitable to more than one species, and it is here that an inquiline may appear. The evolu-

Man and wolves. Paleontological investigation indicates that the dog has been domesticated for some sixty thousand years. The commensalism leading to this domestication must have lasted many times as long.

The black-footed ferret, *Mustela nigripes,* is endangered with extinction because of the activities of humans in destroying prairie dog colonies. The prairie dog, which is simply a colonial ground squirrel, competes with beef cattle for grazing privileges and has been largely eradicated in many areas by trapping and poisoning. The resulting limitation of range prevents the inquiline-ferret from maintaining the healthy gene pool necessary for propagation of its kind.

tion of an inquilinistic symbiosis requires, in addition to a nest-builder, a potential tenant whose form and habits enable it to coexist with its host. Not only must the constructions of the host provide some advantage to the tenant, but the tenant itself must escape the attention of the host—attention that could result in eviction or death.

Inquilinisms may be opportunistic or obligate in nature. An opportunist inquiline may live independently of its host structure, but it seeks such structures out and utilizes them by preference. Obligate inquilinism occurs when for some reason the environment outside the nest becomes hostile, and so the inquiline is obliged to remain in its landlord's home to survive. Among the colonies of prairie dogs, certain snakes and owls may adopt a burrow or two; they are found elsewhere, but there are more of them around prairie dog colonies, where safe burrows are to be had for free. In these same burrows, however, a handsome weasel called the black-footed ferret lives by necessity rather than for mere convenience.

Because weasels are small and agile, they are able to penetrate the burrows of the small mammals on which they prey. These little predators are forced by their size to inhabit areas where there is abundant cover beneath which they may remain safe from larger hunters such as cats and owls. When they forsook the heavy cover of the forest and scrub for the open grassland habitat of prairie dogs, the ancestors of black-footed ferrets were forced to take cover in the burrows of their prey for their own safety, thus becoming obligate tenants of prairie dog colonies.

The earliest inquilinisms probably evolved when animals first began burrowing. Such forms as filter-feeders and sediment-eating worms, exca-

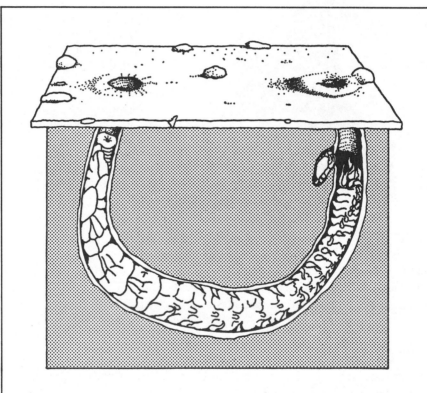

A modern annelid filter-feeder of genus *Chaetopterus*, which constructs a U-shaped tube beneath the mud of tidal flats. The animal gathers particulate waterborne food with a mucus sac secreted at its anterior end (*left*), and excretes through the other end of the tube. At the excretory end, a small crab has adopted the part of inquiline, preying upon organisms attracted by the fecal swell.

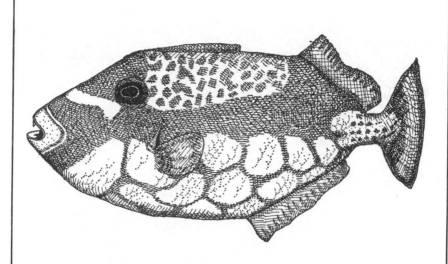

A triggerfish, one of the thousands of inquilines of colonial corals. The animal is so called because of the triggerlike arrangement of bones permitting it to lock a sharp defensive spine in place on its back. Its teeth are adapted to the crushing of coral skeletons in its search for food, and its bright markings announce its presence in territorial matters.

vating the bottom of the seas, found themselves sharing their new spaces with innumerable lesser animals. Utilizing food uncovered by the activities of their hosts and protected from predation by the burrows themselves, these early opportunists proliferated and flourished.

The first building above ground was probably done by animals with solid glandular secretions, such as shells. In such individuals there could be no true inquilinism; a sharer of the shell of a mussel would probably be parasitizing the mollusk. But among the colonial corals, the mass secretion of skeletal matter quickly became the foundation for one of the world's most complex ecological structures, the coral reef. Coral reefs are vast communities of inquilines and provide energy and space for thousands of species of animals of nearly every living phylum. Some species of reef inquilines, such as certain clown- and triggerfish, are specialized to such a degree that they cannot reproduce if separated from the specific reef of their origin.

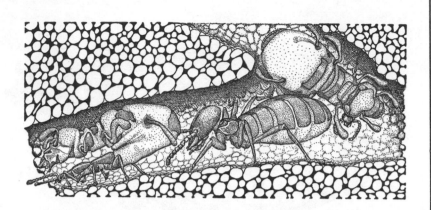

Cross section of a termitary tunnel showing two rove beetles and a host termite (*center*). The dorsal view of the beetle on the right shows the animal's real head and two of its legs protruding from beneath the great abdomen. Like prehistoric human hunters wearing stag skins and antlers to infiltrate herds of prey deer, these beetles infiltrate their hosts' termitaries through disguise.

During the late Mesozoic era (between one hundred seventy million and one hundred million years ago), certain types of cockroaches started on the path that was to culminate in the complex nest-building societies that we now call termitaries. Specialized by a curious mutualism with microbes living in their intestines, these insects were able to digest cellulose, the skeletal matter of woody plants. Burrowing inside dead wood, the roaches carried their eggs with them, after the manner of all roaches, until they hatched. Their offspring acquired the cellulose-digesting microbes necessary for the eating of dead wood by eating their parents' fecal matter. Behavior that increased the likelihood of the youngsters' eating fecal material served to increase the chances that these young would live to reproduce. Some roaches developed feeding patterns in which feces were offered directly to their offspring; this relationship between generations became the foundation for the evolution of caste systems and the ultimate success and diversification of the termites.

As the colonies of termites increased in complexity, they provided microhabitats suitable to the needs of many other small animals. Evolving and diversifying along with their landlords, these beetles, flies, bugs, roaches, springtails, bristletails, millipedes, mites, spiders, and crustaceans are unique to termitaries and vary according to the species and location of their hosts. All inquilines must develop characteristics which protect them from the defenses of their landlords. Termitary inquilines use means ranging from bodily armor to attractive or concealing odor; some develop qualities resembling those of the landlord termites to the point where the landlords cannot tell the inquilines from legitimate colony members. An extreme example of this identification with the host occurs in a rove beetle of the genus *Coatonachthodes* whose abdomen resembles to an extraordinary degree the body of its African landlord termite. Complete with "legs," "antennae," and the proper colonial odor, this abdomen is a splendid evolutionary achievement, a salute to insect adaptability.

Some of the wasps evolved social systems, and among their descendants are the ants and bees, whose societies have enabled them to become the most numerous of insects in many places. Their wide variety and worldwide range have provided habitats for hundreds of species of tenant animals, from butterflies to pseudoscorpions. Inquilines of ants, bees,

A thysanuran insect (*left center*) traveling with army ants. These ants construct no underground dwelling but move in vast numbers across Central American forest floors in search of insect prey. The little thysanuran possesses odors matching the colonial odor of the ants and scavenges from the kills made by its host colony. The thysanuran also finds protection from predators by remaining an inquiline and is never found separate from army ants as an adult.

termites, and other social insects may function as scavengers within the colony; they may groom their hosts, inducing them to regurgitate food; they may lick host secretions or follow host trails to food; they may feed on aphids or fungi symbiotic with the host, or on stored foodstuffs, or even on the materials of the nest itself. A few inquilines of social insects prey on the host larvae or adults, and some become true parasites, laying eggs on their hosts or clinging to their bodies as ectoparasites.

The most recent social builder, and the provider of the greatest variety of potential microhabitats, is *Homo sapiens.* Combining the flexible behavior characteristic of mammals having social habits, the use of inorganic tools, and information exchange (language) of great intricacy, humans may construct entire landscapes for themselves from nearly any earthly environment.

It is likely that the earliest humans were nomads, living largely on the energy stored in large mammalian herbivores and supplementing this diet with almost anything else that was organic, nonpoisonous, and within reach. They would even eat grass seed, if they couldn't get anything else, and so they discovered how to cultivate grasses. Humans suddenly changed from occasional predators, limited in population by the nature of their food, to primary consumers sharing a new mutualism with the grasses they maintained. Instantly, human populations expanded from a few bands of wandering hunters into vast herds—I can think of no better word—of herbivores, creating settlements of hundreds of grass-eaters on areas of land that might at best have supported one or two dozen of their nomadic ancestors.

With the increase in population of this instant herbivore came the need for more food—more acreage, more room. Humans, for the first time in their few million years, came into direct competition with a large number of other life forms. They overflowed the niche for which they were originally designed, invading and destroying the niches of thousands of other species. Razing forests, they replaced them with fields of their symbiotic grasses. Burning meadows, they replaced them with towns and cities. Humans domesticated other animals, requiring more grasses and more acreage with which to maintain them. To protect these domesticated animals, they destroyed potential predators, accelerating the conversion of the original landscape.

In a short ten thousand years, the change in human eating habits has terminated one world and created another. With the advent of large-scale human transformation of the biological cosmos came the creation of new, impoverished ecosystems whose biomasses became concentrated in

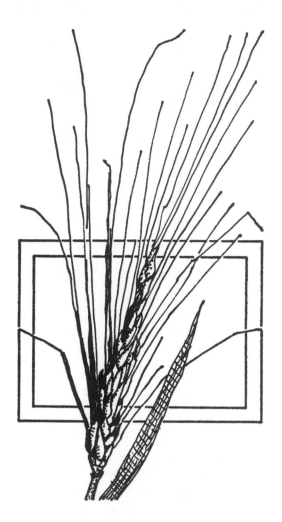

A wild grass of the genus *Secale,* ancestor of cultivated rye. Mutualism between grasses and human beings laid the foundation for the evolution of highly complex human societies and the consequent spaces for inquilines.

the few plants and animals designed to feed or otherwise provide for human beings. By eliminating competing predators and rendering many habitats unsuitable for wild animals, human activity tended to turn ancient and vigorously complex biomes or ecological communities into relative deserts. This process of conversion has resulted in the segregation from the overall living system of an artificial energy-distribution system based on the photosynthetic capabilities of domestic plants and oriented around the requirements of one species—Man. We call this artificial system, which is now global in scope, anything from "civilization" to the "human endeavor." Whatever it is called, the artificial system is based on the exclusion of any organism that may compete with us for the biomass we attempt to imprison.

Life, though, is clever and quick. "Nature abhors a vacuum," they say, and as humans created new spaces in the living system, other animals arose to exploit those spaces. A few species actively profited from proximity to human activity, finding in it a combination of increased food availability and reduced predation. Because of the recent appearance and momentary duration of humanity's agricultural and building activity, most of these animals remain opportunists able to resume a wilderness existence in suitable habitats. But humans have migrated since they acquired their inquilines, producing new societies in habitats far removed from their native lands. The inquilines, following, become limited to the sphere of human activity by the hostility of the surrounding community. They are obliged to remain our tenants in many cases, and they become even more intimate with us as we invade new lands.

In some of the chapters to come, we will deal with aspects of our inquilines that cause them to be understood largely in terms of their monetary cost to human societies. In many cases they compete directly with us for food and space, infesting our storehouses, our homes, even our bodies, with unwanted organic matter. Our inquilines have become economic considerations to us, and it is as economic entities that they appear in much of the literature. The word "economics" is derived from the Greek root *oikos,* "household." Economics is a body of speculation considering the commerce of humanity, which is seen as the exchanges between the various human "households" (nations, corporations, individuals, and so forth) of any imaginary or real commodity of significance to the artificial system.

Derived from the same Greek root is the word "ecology." Ecology is a body of inquiry considering no more nor less than the distribution of matter, energy, and space through the earthly living system, our household at large. It can readily be seen that economics is but a minuscule wrinkle in the study of ecology, just as the artificial system is but a momentary anomaly in the process of organic evolution. Indeed, strictly economic thinking subjects us to illness and inconvenience in much the same way as does our appendix, a similar remnant of more primitive times; it can, for instance, be accurately stated that the pursuit of various economic goals or doctrines is directly responsible for the great wars of the twentieth century and the present despoiling of the planetary surface.

I have tried to avoid the error of the narrow economic viewpoint in favor of a broader consideration of ourselves and our inquilines based on our physical and behavioral characteristics and our relative places in the living system. While our inquilines are cousins to us in the biological family, they parted from our stock long ago and have taken strange and devious routes to return to us, millions of years later, transformed. Each of these tenants joined us because its design somehow fitted one of the gaps we created when we took the wheel of evolution. Each species is a history, a set of characteristics representative not only of itself, but of its family, of its class, of all life. Our inquilines are message-bearers from the parent crystal, simultaneously alien and familiar. Their wildness is made possible *by* the artificial system, not in spite of it.

So in a sense this book is not solely an examination of our tenants. It is also a look in a mirror of ourselves, a consideration of our history and our ways, perhaps a criticism of them. I hope that it will spark some curiosity about the affairs of these fascinating and annoying creatures and about the factors that endear us to them. In turn, the inquilines offer us a look at the strategy of the living system itself, the study of which strategy we call ecology. Ecology, then, is what this book, and you and I, are about.

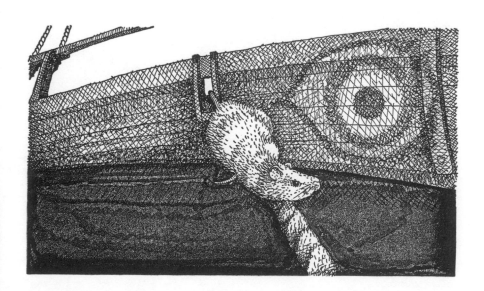

1   The House Sparrow

A carpenter of ancient Israel once remarked that "the meek shall inherit the earth." This comment neatly expresses the story of the evolutionary success of the house sparrow, *Passer domesticus,* which arose from humble beginnings to colonize most of the planet. Indeed, the house sparrow is probably the most familiar form of wildlife to the world's billions of city-dwelling people. Its spread across the earth resulted from its original association with the fierce and technologically advanced western European culture, which in a short four centuries managed to bring the Bible, the gun, and the house sparrow to every continent except Antarctica. During this odyssey, *Passer domesticus* has subspeciated into at least seven distinct races and is showing signs of further differentiation as it follows humanity into new environments.

House sparrows are members of the order Passeriformes, the "sparrowlike" or perching birds. Significantly named after its most familiar member, the order includes some fifty-two hundred species representing what are generally considered to be the most evolutionarily advanced of birds. Worldwide in distribution, the Passeriformes are by far the largest and most diverse order of air-breathing vertebrates.

The suborder to which house sparrows belong is called the Oscines, "songbirds," and includes the most familiar birds of yard and garden. As an oscine bird, the house sparrow enjoys the company of more than four

23

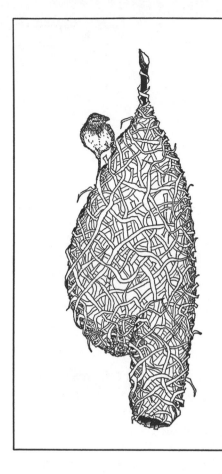

A weaverbird, on the grass nest for which his kind are named. The building of such nests is instinctual; weavers separated from their parents at birth and raised in captivity will build precisely the same kind of nest despite the absence of any learning opportunity.

thousand species, including thrushes, crows, jays, finches, weaverbirds, larks, lyrebirds, wrens, creepers, tits, birds of paradise, warblers, and the ubiquitous starlings who share with the house sparrow much of the human range. The Oscines do not all have a highly developed song, but each of them boasts intricate and specialized vocal apparatus for intricately modulated vocalizing.

The house sparrow was originally classified along with finches, American "sparrows," grosbeaks, and their allies, but more recent research indicates that the sparrows of genus *Passer* are really weavers, members of the family Ploceidae along with about 135 species of sparrow weavers, sociable weavers, cuckoo weavers, whydahs, bishops, swamp weavers, and others. Most weavers inhabit Africa south of the Sahara and southern Asia east to the islands of Bali and Java. Some species have colonized Madagascar and other islands of the Indian Ocean, but the house sparrow is the only weaver to have extended its range significantly beyond these limits.

All of these weavers share certain behavioral characteristics, such as gregarious habits and the building (where conditions require it) of elaborate domed nests. Their name is derived from their remarkable architectural talents, and the elegantly woven nests of many species have gained the family worldwide fame. Most weavers literally warp-and-woof a domed nest, some species building vast condominia of carefully woven thatch. House sparrows share the dome-building trait, but in their adopted holes and niches among the buildings of men they tend to omit the dome in favor of the more familiar cup of straw and litter.

House sparrows share the weaverbird trait of dome-building, but when adapting their nests to human habitation, they favor the more familiar cup shape.

Genus *Passer,* which includes all the Old World or "true" sparrows, contains about eleven other species somewhat similar in appearance to Domesticus. Most of these are specialized to ecological niches that have sharply restricted their ranges, but the most familiar of them, the tree sparrow, *Passer montanus,* is native to wooded areas across Eurasia and has been introduced into the midwestern United States, the Philippines, and Australia.

Until agriculture became widespread, the tree sparrow was the dominant form of *Passer* on the Eurasian land mass. Following the retreat of the last glaciers, great forests sprang up across the continent, providing a wide and hospitable range for this arboreal and largely insectivorous bird. Successfully occupying most niches available to weavers in the temperate Eurasian forests, the tree sparrow represented its family there for thousands of years.

During the same era of glacial retreat there appeared along the southern edge of Europe, in the Middle East, and in northern Africa, meadows and prairies supporting herds of grass-eating mammals and other animals dependent on an open-land way of life. In these sunlit lands edging the Mediterranean and its tributary rivers dwelt a close relative of the tree sparrow, a weaver more inclined to eat the seeds of plants and to frequent bright spaces. Restricted from spreading north by the postglacial forests, and from expanding into Africa by the presence there of other weavers entrenched in all suitable habitats, these birds remained limited to a relatively narrow range for thousands upon thousands of their generations. They were a peripheral species, these proto–house sparrows, building spherical nests with neat entrance holes of the bountiful grasses of their homelands, biding their time in that distant spring of the world.

In those days another animal, a mammal, was experiencing a revolution. Along the eastern end of the Mediterranean, human beings were discovering that certain grasses, when properly cared for, could be managed artificially—to feed humans. Barley and wheat, favorites of the grassland sparrows, were the first domesticated grains, and other grasses were adapted to human use as agricultural technology spread into different climates. This new symbiosis between plants and men permitted the formerly nomadic tribes a more sedentary existence, and with increased stability and numbers came an increase in the rate of technological evolution.

So the meadowlands grew as the forests were cut and burned. Maintaining plants not only for themselves but also for their domesticated herbivores, humans expanded their activities northward, westward, and eastward, bringing with them a meadowland ecological community of their own making. The growing farms became new territory for house sparrows at the expense of their relatives in the forests. Not only was the food of men and domestic herbivores also the food of sparrows, but the human buildings provided superb nesting places, their various nooks and crannies obviating the necessity for the ancestral domed nest. With the advance of humanity came the retreat of predators, and with the retreat of predators came great increase in the populations of both humans and sparrows. Ecological fraternal twins, agricultural humanity and the house sparrow spread from their Fertile Crescent birthplace on a journey of ten millennia to see the world.

As agriculture spread, the former range of tree sparrows quickly dwindled. Not so the house sparrow, which, confronted with a variety of new climates and pressures, diversified in form and behavior. *Passer domesticus domesticus* subspeciated along the eastern Mediterranean to produce a variant known as *P. d. biblicus,* the sparrow of Holy Writ, while in the fields of Iberia arose *P. d. hispaniolensis. P. d. italiae* stole seed from Etruscan granaries, and across the Mediterranean *P. d. niloticus* lived among Pharaoh's minions. Among the embryonic civilizations of the Indian subcontinent was born *P. d. indicus,* whose descendants yet peck at the leavings of sacred cattle. House sparrows continued their spread across Asia until 1929, when they first appeared at the mouth of the Amur River on the Soviet Pacific coast, having followed the Trans-Siberian Railroad. This was just about as far as they could go without a helping hand.

The great European emigrations of the fifteenth to the nineteenth centuries paved the way for worldwide expansion of house sparrows. Responsibility for this outbreak rests largely with the ferociously empire-minded British, whose advanced seafaring technology enabled them to spread their cultural and genetic heritage across so much of the planet. Persons of British extraction, stuck in British colonies abroad, became homesick for the sparrows so common in their ancestral lands. For having arranged the planting of sparrows in new nations, these persons are memorialized in the common name "English sparrow."

Inhabitants of the city of Brooklyn seem to have been among the earliest Americans to express the strange desire to be surrounded by house sparrows. In the cities of Europe house sparrows were scavengers of seed from horse droppings and gleaners of scrap, and otherwise useful in a minimal sort of way. Further, their constant chirping and ever-present fat forms made them a part of Europe's very architecture, so nostalgic Brooklynites decided to see to it that America was equally blessed with such an inquiline to accompany Man and to glorify Him.

The Brooklyn Institute, an organization of public-spirited New Yorkers interested in the progress of their city, set up the first committee to oversee the seeding of North America with *Passer domesticus*. A Mr. Nicholas Pike was appointed chairman of the committee, and in 1850 he purchased eight pairs of house sparrows from England. These birds were maintained over the winter by the Institute and released in the spring of the next year; however they were too few, and the entire planting disappeared. The following year the Institute allotted two hundred dollars for the importation of a number of British songbirds, including house sparrows. At this time Pike was appointed to a diplomatic post in Portugal and en route to Lisbon personally oversaw the purchase of this shipment of birds. After arriving in Brooklyn, twenty-five pairs of sparrows were released along the East River. The rest wintered under the care of the Institute and in the spring of 1853 were released on the grounds of Brooklyn's Greenwood Cemetery, a name that will forever live in ecological infamy. In this bit of suburban greenery reserved for the disposal of dead humans, America's first permanent colony of house sparrows multiplied—and spread.

In 1854, meddlesome bird lovers in Portland, Maine, released more pairs of sparrows. Citizens of New Haven imported some of their own in 1857, and in 1858 a few sparrows destined for Peacedale, Rhode Island, escaped in Boston, where they established a short-lived foothold. The remaining portion of this shipment was successfully planted in Peacedale, but Bostonians, who had gotten their own dose of sparrow fever, imported more of the birds, which this time took permanent hold. In 1869 the city of Philadelphia released a thousand sparrows to brighten the streets of the City of Brotherly Love, starting a sorry chain of events that led ultimately to a Pennsylvania law making it desirable to "kill or in any way destroy" the descendants of the planting.

Sparrows had become an American fad. Breeders sprang up to supply the new market for the birds, lavishing fine food and tender care on their charges, preparing elegant quarters for the winter, and releasing birds in areas precleared of predators and provided with nesting boxes. In the cities of the new nation the sparrows found an earthly heaven. The ever-present horse droppings, livestock and poultry feed, and general garbage, coupled with the vast fields of grain surrounding the cities, made these formerly sparrowless places perfect breeding grounds for the invaders. From a few thousand square kilometers in 1875, the range of the house sparrow in the United States expanded by some 1,340,000 square kilometers in the subsequent eleven years. This was only the beginning.

Countless private citizens contributed to the spread of house sparrows by trapping acclimated birds and releasing them in distant towns. Enthusiasts in Texas, Ohio, Utah, Missouri, Georgia, and other states acquired breeding stock, and by 1875 *P. domesticus* was breeding in San Francisco. Nova Scotia, Quebec, and Ontario staged releases of sparrows, and a seeding in Havana in 1850 brought them to Cuba. From the United States house sparrows expanded their range into Mexico, and introductions into Brazil and Venezuela between 1872 and the turn of the century resulted in their overrunning much of South America. Planting in Australia from 1863 to 1872 spread house sparrows through all of that continent except for the dry west and the hot, moist north. In the 1860s they were introduced to New Zealand, spreading thence unaided to Norfolk and the Campbell Islands, 720 and 560 kilometers respectively from the New Zealand mainland.

Accidental transmission around the world facilitated the spread of these adaptable birds. The Indian subspecies stowed away on ships, reaching Durban on the east coast of South Africa and moving on through all of southern Africa, Zambia, and Malawi. Indigenous weavers held their own in the wilderness, but where European activity was most intense, such aboriginal weavers as the Cape and East African sparrows were forced to retreat before their pugnacious northern cousins—much as native African humans were forced to give way to the European invaders. Sparrows attracted to shipboard livestock pens and feed bins managed to gain access to islands where they were able to settle with little or no competition. Thus, stowaway sparrows in sheep pens established themselves in the Falkland Islands from ports in South America.

Everywhere they went house sparrows intensified the ecological disruption of native habitats wrought by European technologies. In the United States, such animals as cliff and tree swallows, martins, and bluebirds were displaced by the aggressive sparrows, which evicted them from nesting holes and competed with them for food. Sparrows are fierce out of proportion to their size, forcing birds of comparable habits to move elsewhere or starve. Their world travels have brought them into contact with all manner of disease, so that they have become recognized vectors of poultry and pigeon parasites, equine encephalitis, and other disorders of birds and mammals. Having established themselves beyond the fondest dreams of their importers a century ago, house sparrows have achieved the status of pest in the United States and around the world. "Pest" is an archaism for disease, as in "pestilence," and among many humans the house sparrow occupies the level of esteem of psoriasis, ringworm, or athlete's foot. Some people have gone so far as to call them "weeds of the air," placing them in the broad category of things not directly useful to humans, things that are customarily destroyed.

Such persons, however, are probably members of that class which projects a future earth inhabited solely by humanity and hydroponic food plants. They fall prey to a brand of thinking that is surely lethal in the end. There is a certain grandeur in the sudden success of *P. domesticus,* a grandeur perhaps paralleling our own (very likely temporary) bloom. There are things around us to which we are but a flash in the pan, to which Rome and America are evanescence personified.

There is a lesson of humility for us in the nature of house sparrows, in birdness itself. To share this lesson I'd like to step back in time, say a couple of hundred million years, to an era when other beings were lords of the planet and when our own kind was but a twinkle in the eye of a brown bug-eater at the roots of a tree. The shape of lands and life was different then, but there were things of birdkind, sparrowkind, and their magnificence haunts us still.

The idea that birds are no less than flying dinosaurs is astounding to me. It is stupefying, as if Tutankhamen were to speak, as if one of those lost civilizations were really to turn up along some forgotten Amazon headwater. Yet it is so; the shriek of a sparrow echoes the Mesozoic as surely as do the unspeakable bones in the halls of paleontology at the American Museum of Natural History. You might think I'd have out-grown this amazement by now, having known it for years. It's an obsession, though, visiting me in my sleep. All those sparrows out there are cousins of *Antrodemus* the allosaur. Keep on eye on them.

A lot of us were brought up with the idea that dinosaurs were vast, cold-blooded hunks of meat whose brains were much too small. We believed that they were so badly designed that the tiny mammals of their era finally overcame them. But there is little notice taken of the fact that mammals coexisted with dinosaurs for some ninety million years, remaining insignificant in size and impact while dinosaurs occupied nearly every ecological niche available to air-breathing vertebrates. And a lot of folk sharing this Disneyesque view of dinosaurs as doomed from the start seem to choose to ignore some significant relative timespans.

The dinosaurs were the dominant vertebrates on this planet for at least one hundred and sixty million years. To gain perspective on this, reflect that mammals have been dominant for only seventy million years at the outside, and that they never radiated into the air as successfully as the dinosaurs did. (Diversification into new ecological niches is called "radiation" by evolutionary biologists.) Furthermore, humans, the "paragon of animals," have been around as occasional tool-users for a scant *five* million years (at most), and *Homo sapiens,* Man the Wise himself, has existed for one million or less. And at the time of this writing the highly developed human technology, coupled with the underdeveloped human evolutionary sense, seems capable of sending Man the Wise down the path of Stegosaurus to oblivion.

It is not difficult to see, then, that the dinosaurs were far from the animal Edsels our cartoonists make them out to be. They are in fact the most successful terrestrial vertebrates so far. The traditional view of dinosaurs as cold-blooded lizards raises an inevitable question: What is responsible for their immense success? How could such hypertrophied "reptiles" have survived for so long, through ecological changes that would surely have eliminated any real reptile?

The answer to this lies in the fact, only recently understood, that dinosaurs were *not,* metabolically speaking, reptiles. They were archosaurians, "rulers of reptiles." Although they shared enough of the skeletal structure of modern reptiles to have confused early paleontologists, they were metabolically akin to the birds. They were endotherms, "warm-blooded" animals, like ourselves and like house sparrows.

How on earth do we know *that?*

Many dinosaurs were of graceful, agile build. Early dinosaurs were nearly all lightly built bipeds, and this speedy frame enabled them to occupy almost any habitat available to modern mammals of comparable mass. But no living reptile shows such grace; the reptilian metabolism does not permit long-leggedness. Those few modern lizards able to rise onto their hind legs are tiny animals which do so only for short bursts of speed. Furthermore, the larger a reptile, the shorter, proportionately, are its legs. This is in keeping with the inability of such animals to regulate their body temperatures without the aid of external factors—sun and shade. If a large lizard were to stand up and run, its muscles would overheat it in minutes. It would collapse and be eaten. But there were dinosaurs weighing several tons, built to move birdlike on two legs, and fast.

Also, there is evidence in the composition of some Mesozoic sediments and in the former wanderings of the earth's magnetic poles to suggest that dinosaurs inhabited cold polar lands where no lizard can go. Even in temperate climates, lizards as large as dinosaurs would be incapacitated by the range of temperature. Cold reptiles wind down like clocks, to be rewound only by the application of heat. How could a snake chase about in the snow?

There is additional evidence of the birdlike metabolism of the dinosaurs in the structure of their bones. Microscopic examination of cross sections of dinosaur bone indicates that a system of Haversian canals, similar to those present in bird and mammal bones, enabled dinosaurs to maintain a high metabolic rate. These canals, which permit the rapid calcium/phosphate exchange necessary to endothermic metabolism, are not present in reptile bone, which is relatively solid in cross section and often exhibits growth rings resulting from seasonal hibernation.

Examining entire deposits ("faunas") of fossil dinosaurs, we are sometimes able to calculate a rough ratio between the biomasses of populations of herbivores and of the carnivores that preyed on them. This ratio indicates to a certain extent the amount of food a carnivore needs to remain functional. Because ectotherms, or "cold-blooded" animals, such as lizards, require far less prey to maintain their relatively sluggish metabolic rates than endotherms do, their herbivore/carnivore mass ratio is significantly lower. Dinosaur herbivore/carnivore ratios are as high as or higher than those of modern mammals, suggesting that things in the Mesozoic were not as they have seemed to several generations of paleontologists.

Feathers, with which house sparrows are covered, seem to have evolved long before feathered flight—as bodily insulation. A feather is essentially a frayed, circular scale, and it is likely that many smaller dinosaurs were covered with contour or filo-feathers much like those of modern birds. Among the pterosaurs, the "winged lizards" of nineteenth-century paleontology, there is evidence of hairy body covering, and a light, gliding bipedal dinosaur from the Jurassic has been christened *Archaeopteryx,* "Old Wing," because it is the earliest known animal with quill feathers like those of modern birds. It is a short step from small dinosaurs, with scales modified to enable a gliding existence like that of flying squirrels, to flying birds. The dinosaurs took that step.

Other archosaurians had taken to the air long before the appearance of birds. The pterosaurs ruled the sky for many millions of years, soaring on batlike wings of sheets of skin supported on the bones of the arm and one finger. But a tear in this sheet of leather meant the end of a pterosaur; the wing could not heal and pterosaurs were poor walkers, helpless on the ground. The pterosaurs, in competition with the first feathered fliers, became extinct and left no descendants.

The advent of feathered flight surfaces meant that the dinosaurs possessing them were in little danger of tearing their wings. Feathers part over obstacles, and even the loss of a few wing feathers is quickly repaired. A house sparrow can replace a missing primary feather in twelve days, with

Restoration of *Archaeopteryx,* closely related to the ancestors of today's birds.

an average growth rate of 4 millimeters per day. Moreover, birds, retaining the bipedal agility of their terrestrial ancestors, were able to run efficiently enough so that grounded birds could escape predation for a time. The original birds—the feathered dinosaurs—superseded pterosaurs much as their descendants would later relegate bats to a largely nocturnal existence.

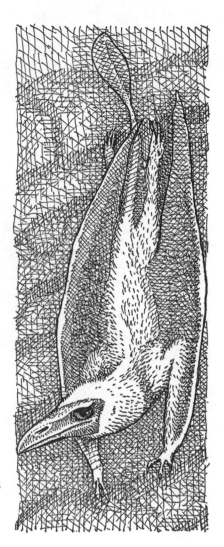

Right: A pterosaur hanging from a seaside cliff. The claws on the wings indicate that the animal may have climbed about on all fours.

Thus the dinosaurs conquered the air, and in so doing they escaped the ecological changes that caused the extinction of their terrestrial relatives.

Dinosaurs are undergoing a rearrangement by modern taxonomists from their original reptilian classification. Some people now suggest that the higher vertebrates are more logically organized in the family tree according to their metabolic structures, rather than according to gross bone structure as they have been classified for more than a century. In this plan a new class is created, Archosauria, to include the existing crocodilians (which have a four-chambered heart and highly developed behavioral characteristics reminiscent of birds), the extinct pterosaurs, and, in subclass Dinosauria, the dinosaurs and birds. In this scheme, reptiles such as the living lizards and snakes remain unchanged in classification, as do mammals.

House sparrows, then, are dinosaurs. In the dusty flocks of street and alley runs the blood of movie monsters, crocodiles, and *Tyrannosaurus rex.* Consider the sparrow with respect, not only for its ability to utilize Man the Wise as habitat, but as a mark of the ultimate success of the dinosaurs. If you can get very close—if you can catch one, or have a good glass with which to watch one—look at the scales on its feet, the neat balance at the hip. It is perpetually in motion, the epitome of hungry, feverish need. A Mesozoic awareness, sharp eyes hinting of unimaginable time. A flock of such creatures should make anyone's day.

House sparrows are amalgams of senses and directions so different from ours as to conjure up science-fiction images of consciousness from beyond the solar system. All the television writers and movie producers on the planet seem unable to cook up a finer Alien Being than the sparrow scrapping for a bit of grilled cheese sandwich on the streets of Los Angeles. Recalling that they are made of precisely the same stuff as ourselves, that we are cousins, we may find it interesting to enter the world of a sparrow for a time, to see where life can take itself.

Flight! For discussing birds the word must be accompanied by an exclamation point. Flying is the avian *sine qua non,* all physical and behavioral functions having been adjusted to the use of air as the prime medium of locomotion. It may be said that sparrows solve all their problems by flying away from them, and to that end they represent an approximation of perfection—measured by their biological success, of course.

A careful look out the window at a few sparrows will reveal a thing that I find fairly dazzling: The birds handle gaseous air with their entire bodies as we might manipulate stone or clay. Unlike humans, who roar through the air inside dartlike projectiles, sparrows and their relatives hold the air with feather fingers, cling to it, mold it. One wonders whether they don't *see* it, whether there aren't senses enabling them to perceive the air in masses as we do floors and walls. A sparrow streaks across a hundred meters of air, swings across a final bit of the gas like Tarzan on a vine, and drops onto a wire without even wiggling it! Hanging on the air, the bird can reach through a tiny hole to grab a bit of suet with its beak, without touching the sides of the opening in which the fat is concealed. To these animals the air seems as solid as earth, as real as any stairway seems to us.

The most immediately evident tool for this aerial art is the feather, a structure so perfectly designed for flight that it has become synonymous with buoyance in our thought. Derived from the scales of ancestral reptiles, feathers for the purpose of bodily insulation probably appeared among the first endothermic archosaurians. Among nonflying animals, the modified scales provided insulation from changes in temperature only, probably retaining the simple form earlier described as the "frayed scale." It was only in response to the requirements of flight that the diverse and highly specialized feathers of modern birds appeared.

Because feathers are made of the same keratin (horn) as are scales and hair, they are essentially dead structures. However, as flight surfaces they seem alive and self-healing. The structure of a mature wing feather consists mainly of the central shaft and an airfoil surface called the vane. The vane is composed of parallel barbs springing diagonally from the shaft, each barb locked to its neighbor by a system of barbules equipped with hooks. The barbules from neighboring barbs interlock perpendicular to one another, providing in their millions a surface of surprising strength and resilience. Thus a split vane, when manipulated by its owner, tends to snap its barbules back perpendicular to one another and lock instantly in position, "healing" the split. This manipulation of the flight feathers occurs during preening, when the sparrow takes great care to examine all vanes for splits.

Because of the necessity for near-perfect feather condition in flight, the house sparrow spends hours a day searching through, twisting, adjusting, dusting, and otherwise preening its equipage. At the base of the bird's tail is an oil gland from which a water-repellent and lubricating ointment may be applied to preserve the feathers, and baths of both water and dust discourage to some extent the many small animals that utilize the coat of the house sparrow as a home.

Watching the growth of one of the wing feathers of a sparrow reveals in a way the transition from scales to true flight surfaces. Protected by a very thin horn sheath called the epitrichium, the primordial feather is little more than an outgrowth of the bird's epidermis wrapped around a core of blood vessels providing nourishment for growth. Initially, this epidermal knob differentiates to produce a ring of rapidly growing keratinous matter that is to become the main structure of the feather. Early in the process, one area of the ring tends to grow faster than the rest; this will ultimately

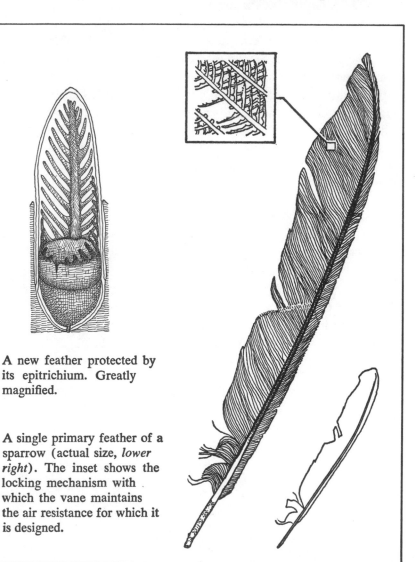

A new feather protected by its epitrichium. Greatly magnified.

A single primary feather of a sparrow (actual size, *lower right*). The inset shows the locking mechanism with which the vane maintains the air resistance for which it is designed.

be the shaft of the feather. The rest of the ring begins to produce corrugations along its rim, and these rapidly differentiate to become the barbs of the feather. As the central shaft grows longer, the barbs are carried out from the original ring, which has become the growing root of the feather.

From the "frayed scale" has arisen a whole gallery of feather variations equipping the sparrow with the most perfectly adapted epidermal covering known. In addition to the vaned, or contour, feathers just discussed, the bird possesses down feathers, with which it maintains its high body temperatures on even the coldest of nights. Movable as all feathers are, these structures may be compressed to release excess heat, or fluffed full of air spaces to provide insulation. The eyes and nostrils of the house sparrow are protected with bristles which are simply barbless feathers, and certain similarly reduced feathers in other parts of the body form part of the systems for reading air currents. Except for its beak, eyes, and feet, the sparrow is completely covered with feathers. It is this versatile coat, unique to birds, that provides them with the air-consciousness responsible for their success.

This air-consciousness is manifested for the bird through sensory systems comparable in their intricacy to those responsible for our own hand-eye-brain coordination. Perhaps most obvious of these is the tactile equipment of the feathers, responsible for the sculpting of air that is the sparrow's flight. Around the follicles of the bird's primary flight feathers, for instance, are high concentrations of Herbst corpuscles, microscopic sensors of touch and vibration. Similar in structure to the Pacinian (touch) corpuscles in humans, Herbst corpuscles register the interaction of pinion and air with such sensitivity that some birds may be able to "hear" sounds with them, catching vibrations on the broad surfaces of their feathers.

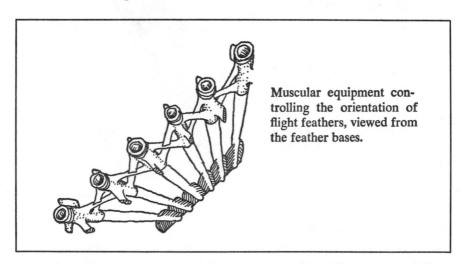

Muscular equipment controlling the orientation of flight feathers, viewed from the feather bases.

Coupled with the enormous sensitivity of the flight feathers is their muscular equipment. Each quill may be elevated, depressed, and rotated; as a group the flight feathers may be spread or drawn together in a solid plane, and the shape and mass of the wings may be shifted to suit conditions and desire. In response to information from the acute sense of balance provided by its semicircular canals, the sparrow changes shape to fit the task at hand. Such incredibly complex and keen perception of the air's force on tens of flight feathers, multiplied by and integrated with the input from the semicircular canals, must produce a mental construct of vivid solidity, a dimension of mass and force that colors much of the sparrow's consciousness. And that isn't all.

The eyes of a sparrow are such as to put our own magnificent sight to shame. Traveling at the heights and speeds they do, sparrows require an acuity and color sensitivity that permits the spotting of a seed of millet in the grass while flying 3 meters above the ground at 20 kilometers per hour, keeping watch for hawks, and evading trees and buildings. To borrow even a sparrow's eye, let alone that of one of the diurnal raptorial birds, would be an exercise in "consciousness expansion" beyond the capability of any drug.

We humans are equipped with some of the best eyes available to mammals. Able to distinguish a wide range of color and outfitted with visual acuity unusual for mammals, a human eye is the primary sensor of its possessor. Humans, like birds, live through their eyes, their success so far being largely a result of their excellent vision. But oh, for the eye of a sparrow! An exercise in fine art, the finest that four billion years of evolution could produce. A human eye has perhaps 200,000 visual cells, both rods (light perception) and cones (color perception), per square millimeter of its retinal surface. The sparrow, though, has more than 400,000 cones *alone* per square millimeter, and about the same number of rods. These high concentrations of cells enable the bird to achieve a visual angle of less than 20 seconds. The visual angle is a measurement of visual acuity derived from testing the minimum angular distance at which separate objects may be resolved separately by an eye. The usual healthy human's visual angle is about one minute, only one third as acute as the sparrow's—and the sparrow has an eye whose diameter is less than a quarter of that of the human eye!

Through its eyes, a sparrow perceives more of its environment than through all the rest of its senses combined. The eye of a sparrow is correspondingly large in proportion to its possessor; both the sparrow head and the human head represent about a tenth of their respective body masses, yet the ratio between human eye-to-head masses is about 1 percent and that of the sparrow some 15 to 20 percent. Together, the sparrow's eyes are larger than its brain, and these giant eyes nearly meet at the center of the bird's skull.

Connecting the eyes and brain in both human and bird are the optic nerves. In humans these nerves are bundles of some one million nerve fibers each; the sparrow may have *twice* as many fibers going to the brain from the eye and, in addition, another several thousand efferent or "out-going" nerves carrying impulses from the brain *to* the retina. It is likely that these nerves permit the brain to alter the sensitivity of the retina by causing its cells to discharge more readily. In photographic terms, sparrows can change the ASA of their film as well as the opening of the camera lens!

In addition to control of retinal sensitivity, the sparrow is equipped with a set of filters which enable it to select for wavelengths of light according to the requirements of a given activity. Many of the bird's cone cells are fitted with colored drops of oil, one to a cone; these drops occur in orange, red, green, and yellow and are designed to select and heighten perception of individual colors in contrast to a rapidly moving background. Thus a sparrow searching for yellow seed around a feeder might see this seed flicker like a beacon through the yellow droplets in its retina. And using yellow and red filters, the bird may pierce atmospheric haze much as does a Skylight filter on a camera.

One specialization of the sparrow's eye that does not occur in mammals is the pecten, a pigmented projection from the rear surface of the eyeball. Present in all birds, the pecten is a roughly conical structure reminiscent of the cooling vanes of an air-cooled engine; its function is believed to be the supply of food and oxygen to the eye, which consumes

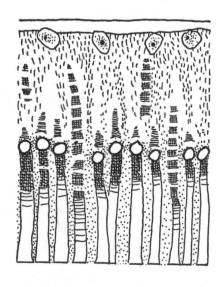

Cross section of sparrow retina, greatly magnified, showing oil droplets (white circles) with which the bird controls color input to its brain.

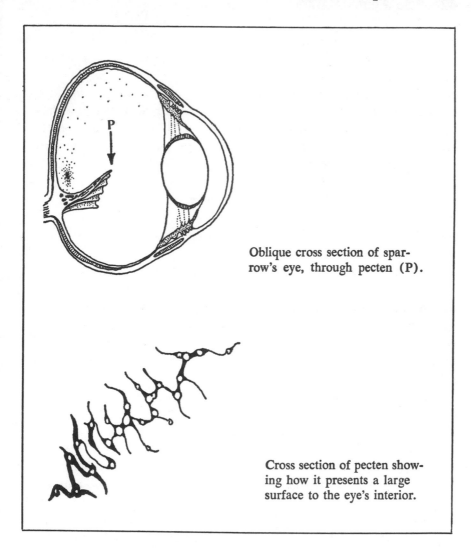

Oblique cross section of sparrow's eye, through pecten (P).

Cross section of pecten showing how it presents a large surface to the eye's interior.

a great deal of energy. The pecten is richly supplied with blood vessels and so constructed as to present a maximum surface area to the inner eye.

Such a splendid eye deserves a pecten! Would that you and I had such eyes, at least for a day. Imagine the ability to see, not only in front of us, but to the side and even a bit to the rear! Such is the sparrow's field of vision, some 300 degrees in extent. What drawings I could make, what marvellous things I could see if I could borrow the eyes from a measly house sparrow! But probably the birds know how to use their staggering visual equipage better than I would. After all, it is an eye for a different mind, and birds' minds are indeed different.

I mentioned earlier that birds fly away from their problems. It seems that the entire avian psychology is based on this escapism, so that problem-solving ability and variability in behavior have been curtailed to a certain extent in its design. With so much of the brain devoted to vision and flying, birds can be said to have been designed to a pattern of "see and flee," other functions being arranged to fit this mold. In invading countless ecological niches, the birds are constrained by the rigors of flight from departing to any significant degree from the avian bodily plan, and the most important adaptations they make are usually inherited with the neural matter of the brain. The physical variability in mammals permits such diverse forms as humans and weasels, but in birds this diversity must be reflected in inborn behavior patterns separating so many similar species one from another.

The vertebrate mind is purpose itself. It is a communications system integrating conditions of the environment with that of the organism, the nucleus, in fact, of the organism/environment field. We humans are specialized in such a way that our lives are long, our young helpless for years while they absorb with hypertrophied brains the information amassed by their elders. It takes a while to fill these huge brains, and a while more to learn how to use them.

But if you were made to live a brief life, live it hard and fast, and then burn out like a falling star, you wouldn't have much time for schooling. If you were a sparrow with, say, a basal metabolic rate of 312 kilocalories per kilogram of your mass per hour (a human adult may have a metabolic rate of *one* kilocalorie per kilogram per hour), and an average life expectancy of about two years in the wild in which to survive and reproduce your kind, you would have to be able to assume your duties quickly and efficiently. Your brain would have to be able to handle all likely contingencies; it would have to contain designed-in behavioral templates to fit the environmental probabilities of your way of life. You would have to be programmed in advance to do the right things, the healthy things, at the right times. Your behavior would be as much inherited as your color, and for the same reason—efficiency in the manufacture of sparrows.

It cannot be said that human beings are devoid of genetic structures governing behavior. Anyone contemplating the barbarous armament of modern nations, anyone, indeed, who has ever experienced a thoughtless rage or infatuation, must be aware of certain ungovernable facets of human behavior as common to all of us as are laughter and tears. But humans, and to a certain extent many of their mammalian relatives, are designed to make use of *possibility*. The higher mammalian brain constructs new

behavior to fit new situations, and its possessor is thus able to cope successfully with environmental conditions of relatively broad scope.

The mind of the bird, dealing as it does in probability rather than
possibility, seems a bit solid-state to those of us mammals who have
adopted the term "birdbrain" for reference to dimmer conspecifics. Confronted with events outside the limits of their genetic preparation, some
birds seem to behave with marvelous stupidity, to the point of killing themselves through preprogrammed but inappropriate responses.

For such a mind we have had to come up with a lexicon of new terms.
Ethology, the science of animal behavior in the natural environment, has
depended for much of its development on the conspicuousness of avian
activity, which permits direct observation in the native habitat. Birds'
seemingly particulate and ritualized behavior has provided the new science
with a good deal of its jargon, inspiring the use of such terms as "innate
releasing mechanism," "discharge," "performance momentum," and others
evocative of automata. However, within the context of its flight-related
limitations, the bird's behavior is among the most advanced known and
often parallels that of mammals in flexibility. The brain of the sparrow, of
course, is the brain of a dinosaur. Its major departures from the original
archosaurian plan as seen in the crocodilian's brain are in areas directly
influencing flight and the associated sense organs. The sparrow's brain is
large for the mass of the entire bird; a male weighing 23.2 grams possesses
a brain of 1.03 grams mass, some 4.5 percent of the bodily total. The brain
of a lizard of comparable mass weighs only 0.54 percent of the animal's
total mass, that of a deer mouse about 2.7 percent. The sparrow's large
brain reflects the rapid and efficient nervous integration necessary for such
a superb flier, in addition to providing storage for the complex inherited
behavior sequences that govern much of the bird's life.

Bird and mammal brains are elaborations of the reptilian form from
which they both descended. However, the mammalian brain exhibits traits
that are associated with its fundamentally smell-oriented nature, in that
mammals evolved as creatures of dank twilights, long-nosed things of the
night in a world dominated by active diurnal archosaurians. The large
mammalian cerebral cortex in particular is derived from areas of the
primitive brain associated with olfaction; this is true even of the visually
oriented higher primates such as ourselves, whose cerebral cortices are
among the largest and most complex known. The mammalian cerebral
cortex, of course, is the Gray Matter, seat of consciousness, source of the
curiosity (nosiness) and pride of our kind.

However, in birds, particularly higher birds such as the house spar-

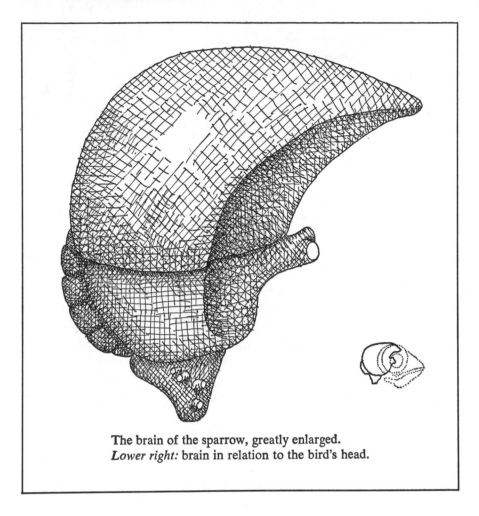

The brain of the sparrow, greatly enlarged.
Lower right: brain in relation to the bird's head.

row, the cortex is reduced to a smooth integument coating only part of the upper surface of the cerebral hemispheres; this in part reflects the reduced importance of olfaction in flying animals and paves the way for a relatively fixed behavioral repertoire. The little sparrow cortex seems to be mainly a repository for conditioned behavior and is not connected to the spinal cord as in mammals, thus sharply limiting the bird's "conscious" control of bodily movement. Mirroring this limitation is the great development of portions of the sparrow's spinal cord, suggesting that many of the complex motions associated with locomotion are integrated in that organ independent of the brain. This development of the spinal cord reached its maximum among some of the sparrow's Mesozoic terrestrial relatives, in whom the body length was so great that "way stations," in the form of spinal ganglia larger than the animals' brains, coordinated many trunk and limb functions and freed the small brain for whatever diversity may have entered the beasts' genetically ordered lives.

Still, the sparrow's cerebral cortex is capable of storing a vast quantity of conditioned learning. Many readers will have seen trained sparrows that pull strings, push carts, and otherwise manipulate objects in the environment in order to receive a reward of food. Such training is built into the bird in a series of steps, each of which is accompanied by food reinforcements, and reflects little or no actual insight on the part of the performer. The function of insight, or what we might call "intelligence," is relegated to that volume of the sparrow's brain which lies beneath the cortex, the subcortical cerebrum.

This area, comprising the bulk of the cerebral hemispheres, shows several layers, derived from parts of the brain of the sparrow's reptilian ancestors and serving largely similar purposes. The layered portion of the cerebrum is called the corpus striatum, and it is here that more complex and variable avian behavior seems to originate. Much of the volume of the corpus striatum seems given to the storage of inherited behavioral templates, particularly the intricate sequences governing courtship and nesting. Corresponding tracts in mammalian brains are much reduced, proportionately so as the animals become more intelligent.

While most major structures of the brain are shared by both birds and mammals, in birds there appears a portion of the corpus striatum which is not present in mammals, the upper part, or hyperstriatum. Experi-

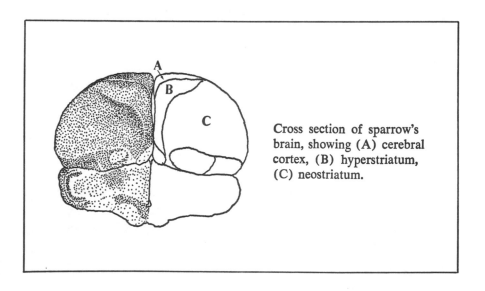

Cross section of sparrow's brain, showing (A) cerebral cortex, (B) hyperstriatum, (C) neostriatum.

ments with many species of birds indicate that parrots, and corvine birds such as crows, jays, and their allies, are the "smartest" in performing tasks of discrimination and counting, some rivaling monkeys in these skills. These tests show that there is a correlation between the volume of the hyperstriatum and the capacity for "understanding," so that we can say that this area controls learning and intelligent, i.e. flexible, behavior, and its strong development in the sparrow has probably to a large extent permitted the animal's exploitation of the variable conditions presented by the human endeavor.

However, in the wilds of New York's Upper East Side, where sparrows are sparrows, behavior is mainly determined by an elegant system of chemical and astronomical chronometers, specific action potentials, releasers, sign stimuli, fixed action patterns, instincts, and discharges, which are as much a part of the physical inheritance of sparrows as is their size. A house sparrow *may* live as long as ten years in the wild, but the more usual life span of two or three years requires that every instant of the animal's life be utilized to the fullest. The system of inherited chronometers and behavioral systems assures by its mechanical reliability that no time is wasted. Even in the longest-lived captive sparrow on record, which died in its twenty-third year, these systems continued functioning to the end—notwithstanding their inappropriateness to the situation of captivity.

Properly maintained, a fertile sparrow egg will produce several others like itself within a period as short as nine months. From a set of molecules, the ultimate in information storage, the clock is started, and in from ten to fourteen days the egg hatches into a helpless, blind, nearly featherless being that must be fully fledged and out of the nest in seventeen more days. To accelerate this process of growth, the parent birds are programmed to feed their offspring a diet radically different from their own in that it consists of some 70 percent animal food, mostly insects, in contrast to the adult diet of only 3 percent insects, the rest vegetation. To facilitate the feeding process, sparrows are designed in such a way that a young sparrow's gaping mouth alone is a signal to the parents for food, and a facsimile in cardboard of an infant sparrow's open beak stimulates the same feeding behavior as does the real thing. This gaping or begging behavior persists among the young for a time after they leave the nest, and a fully fledged juvenile bird may beg at a piece of food too large for it to swallow.

Some twenty-three days after hatching, the sparrow is undergoing the final pneumatization of its skeleton, necessary for the most efficient flight possible. Air sacs reach from the lungs of the young bird into the long wing

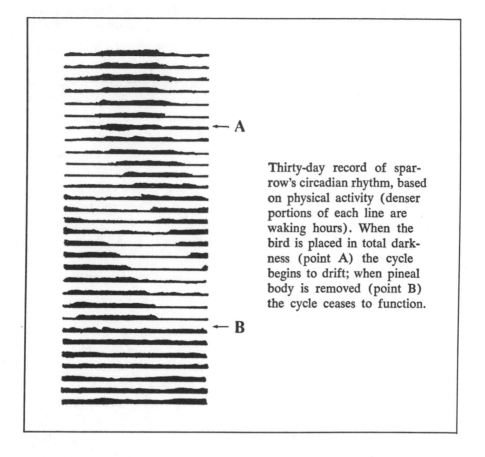

Thirty-day record of sparrow's circadian rhythm, based on physical activity (denser portions of each line are waking hours). When the bird is placed in total darkness (point A) the cycle begins to drift; when pineal body is removed (point B) the cycle ceases to function.

and leg bones and even into the skull, where they lighten the system of struts and braces protecting the eyes and brain. The beak hardens into a nutcracker, provided with ridges and abrasive areas for the manipulation of the seeds and other hard foods that form a large part of the adult diet, and the feathers reach their maximum development at about the time the young bird leaves its parents for a flock of other sparrows its own age.

From the start, the house sparrow is provided by its genes with a clock timed to the passing of the day, a circadian (around-the-day) rhythm operating through blood chemistry to order the bird's time. During this cycle, the temperature and locomotor activity and other metabolic functions are regulated largely by the sun, but a bird kept in total darkness shows a persistence of these cycles independent of the sun's stimulus. Interestingly, when the bird is freed of the sun's input, these cycles begin to show a drift, sliding more and more ahead or astern of the natural daylight cycle. This drift is said to be characteristic of a "free-running" biological clock, and when the darkness-acclimated sparrow is returned to the world of true night and day, it requires several days to adjust to what has become a "jet lag" similar in its effects to that experienced by jet-hopping human diplomats.

Circadian rhythms seem to be governed by the sparrow's pineal body, a nodule of tissue located in the middle of the animal's brain and believed to be a remnant of a median eye, a light receptor present in the top of the skull of many primitive vertebrates, serving to warn them of predation from above. Sparrows from whose brains the pineal body is removed show loss of circadian rhythms even when the birds are kept in natural daylight. Other experiments suggest that the pineal body's content—various enzymes and other compounds basic to metabolic control in animals—changes in response to nerve impulses from the eyes. The pineal body can also be shown to modulate its activity in response to artificial manipulation of the length of the sparrow's external "day." Thus the ancient median eye seems to retain some of its earlier function of integrating behavior to conditions of light and darkness, even though it is buried, a glandular mass, in the brain of the bird.

The young sparrow spends most of its first year in the company of large flocks of unmated sparrows. In the autumn, at the close of the breeding season, adult birds join the flocks and the classic sparrow "migrations" to new sources of food begin. The ripening of certain fruits and cultivated grains are traditional moving-times for house sparrows, and even invasions of locusts, Japanese beetles, or inchworms may attract masses of the birds. At lunch hour on the Pennsylvania Turnpike, flocks of sparrows gather to pick the insects from the radiator grilles of hungry tourists stopped at Howard Johnson's, and house sparrow flocks are aware of all the garbage-emptying, chicken-feeding, and field-sowing in the civilized world.

The institution of the flock is characteristic of many birds, and serves, by the communications system it offers, to make available to the individual bird the eyes and ears of its myriad fellows in the gathering. The sparrow flock is so much more efficient as a food-gathering device that birds of many species join it in times of scarcity, sparrows, starlings, blackbirds, jays, titmice, and others moving in great aggregations in response to news of food and space. Argus-eyed, the flock is also more aware of the proximity of potential predators, an added advantage in autumn when the birds molt and become more vulnerable to predation. Although to the casual observer the flock may seem noisy and disorderly, it is largely unified and performs much of its activity with an amorphous coherence reminiscent of a hungry amoeba.

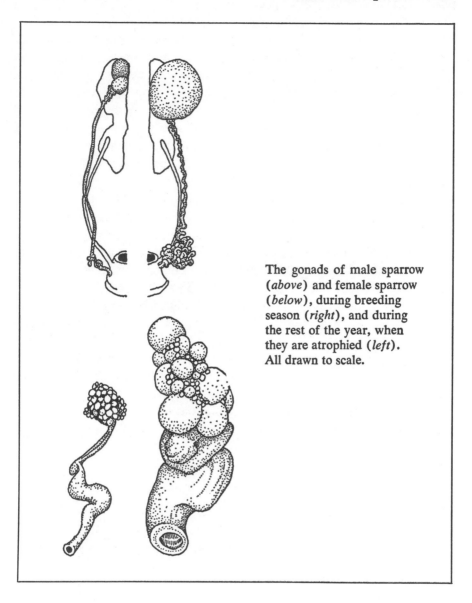

The gonads of male sparrow (*above*) and female sparrow (*below*), during breeding season (*right*), and during the rest of the year, when they are atrophied (*left*). All drawn to scale.

During the entire time it is not engaged in breeding activity, the sparrow has no need for its gonads, male or female. Consequently these organs, which represent a weight debt ill-affordable by a flying animal, must be reduced in mass to provide the maximum lightness possible for the nonbreeding bird. The functioning ovary of a female sparrow (birds use only one ovary—the other, mere excess baggage, atrophied long ago in the evolution of the class) may weigh some 500 milligrams; when the breeding season ends, this massive organ decreases in mass to perhaps 10 milligrams, shrinking by a factor of as much as fifty. In the breeding male, both of whose testes are functional, one testis may weigh 345 milligrams; after the close of the breeding season the same organ may weigh as little as half a milligram. These size cycles are regulated by the pituitary gland of the bird, located at the base of its brain, which produces a variety of hormones in response to the appropriate environmental conditions.

Sparrows, like most other higher birds, are dominated by yearly reproductive cycles as rigid as the seasons of which they make use. The body chemistry of the adult in breeding season is so different from that of the nonbreeding bird as to entirely alter its metabolism and behavior. It can be accurately said that there are two different kinds of house sparrows, breeding and nonbreeding, based on blood content and other measures of body chemistry. The complex and inborn courting, nesting, and other reproductive behavior of house sparrows represents the maximum in compression of information. This behavior is initiated by lengthening days in spring, independent of other factors in the bird's life history, and is largely the same worldwide.

Breeding begins when male sparrows from the winter flocks begin investigating holes, ledges, nest boxes, air conditioners, heating ducts, and almost any other sheltered situation. Simultaneous with this new behavior is the gradual appearance of a black bib, the timing of whose coming is governed by the wearing away of the white tips of last autumn's neck

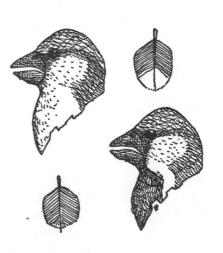

The wearing away of the neck feathers in a male sparrow is responsible for the appearance of his breeding color at the proper time. *Above,* male in autumn, with one neck feather showing white tip. *Below,* same male in spring, white tips worn away.

feathers. This wearing proceeds such that the white-necked autumn bird-of-the-flock becomes a nest-holder badged with office, without undergoing the intervening energy expenditure of a molt.

In many familiar Passeriformes, such as the American robin, the courting male first selects a territory, defending its borders and advertising for a mate with his song and coloring. However, in colonial nesters, such as the weavers, territory outside the nest is meaningless, and the male instead contents himself with a nest site, in which he may pile a bit of debris as a foundation. The courting male may, where space permits, select several nest sites and start a nest in each. After the formation of a pair-bond these extra nests may serve as resting or eating places in addition to the breeding nest.

The classic courtship dance, for the benefit of the unconcerned female sparrow at center.

The pair-bond between a male and female sparrow is predicated upon the male's having selected a suitable nest site. Having selected such a site, the male displays to his peers, shouts his ownership of a home, and begins at the same time to court the ladies. The appearance at a suitable time of a suitably unattached female produces the following sequence of behavior in the male: He approaches the female on the ground, his wings dragging on the earth, his tail held erect, wrenlike, squealing loudly all the while in the manner of a minuscule piglet. He performs a dance, revolving with wings dragging and all the trappings of his machismo displayed to their fullest. If the lady is bought by this behavior, she seizes her suitor by his wing tip and may drag him for a considerable distance across the ground. If she is unready for an attachment, she may respond to the advances of the male by adopting a threat posture and lowering her head to charge her suitor. This naturally serves to intensify his courting, and the squealing of his ardor may attract rival males, up to fourteen simultaneously courting one reluctant lady. A familiar sight in nearly all the world's cities, the spiraling, wing-dragging courtship dance is universal and as much a part of the inborn structure of the sparrow as is the timing of its bib.

The newly mated pair may remain united for life, breeding together year after year, but life for wild house sparrows is short and the widowed quickly bond again.

The male introduces his mate to the nesting site, and together they build the nest. Females ordinarily transport the bulk of the nesting material, while males defend their chosen site from those males that have yet to establish themselves. In exposed situations such as the limbs of trees, the pair will construct a typical domed weaver's nest, but among the edifices of humankind a simple cup usually suffices. Built from straws, strings, aluminum foil, toilet paper, wire, *The New York Times,* and almost anything else the birds can carry, these nests are a fundamental bone of dissension between birds and the superintendents of buildings. Not only humans but birds of other species are inconvenienced by the sparrow's breeding activity, for a male sparrow often evicts the rightful owner of an already constructed nest and moves in on his own. Entire colonies of cliff swallow nests may be inhabited by house sparrows, and the very ranges of many species, such as the Eastern bluebird and house wren, have been much reduced by the pugnacious sparrows.

The sequence of nest-building and breeding in sparrows is rigid and inexorable. Young birds introduced to adults in the nest-building stage may be tossed to the ground from the nest or even incorporated into its structure. When the nest is completed, however, the parents may respond to the gaping of introduced young and rear them with their own. With the enlargement of the birds' gonads for the breeding season comes the adjustment of much of their metabolism to prepare for the taxing weeks ahead. Particularly in the female, whose body must invest so much in the way of nutriment and energy in the production of eggs, the blood shows changes in concentration of sugars, fats, and calcium as the animal changes her diet to make eggs. Both adults are more vulnerable to accident and predation during breeding, and more than half of all house sparrow deaths occur during the three-month or shorter period of breeding with its increased exposure and energy drain. The interaction of circadian clocks and the sparrow's endocrine system results in the sequence of behavior best able to counter this increased adult mortality by the successful rearing of as many young as possible in the allotted time. Differences in sequence or in number of broods tend to reflect the climate prevalent in the adults' breeding range; sparrows in environments with short summers may produce one yearly brood of nine eggs, while those in kinder lands may breed two to four times in rapid succession, laying three or four eggs in a brood.

The built-in chronometers and programming of the modern house sparrow live on largely unaltered from preagricultural times. This intricate behavioral inheritance offers us a window on times long past, and an idea of conditions in which these birds evolved. Sparrow behavior reflects a habitat of temperate climate, one which was warm enough to discourage true migration, but changeable enough to force diversity in eating habits. The colonial nesting habits of the weavers also reflect an open-land way of life in which arboreal nesting situations may have been too few to support many isolated, territorial pairs of birds. A tree that might support one breeding pair of territorial birds may support several tens of pairs of sparrows, each defending only its nest from the others.

It was in this matter of nesting habits that the proto–house sparrows departed from the general grasslands weaver pattern, for they acquired the ability to use varied nesting situations where conditions warranted. This change, reflecting unstable conditions in the savanna's tree-sized flora, liberated the sparrows from the weaver tradition of building highly specialized nests requiring great time and energy expenditure on the part of breeding birds and allowed the use of sites other than trees for nest-building. Suitable nests prepared by other species, as we have seen, became targets for male sparrows establishing pair-bonds, and the judicious choice of spots in close proximity to colonies of stinging insects or large predators such as eagles permitted breeding sparrows a degree of protection unavailable to their less adaptable cousins.

We can readily see that the proto–house sparrows were already admirably equipped for exploiting the nesting sites provided by the activities of early agriculturalists. In keeping with the flexibility of their nesting behavior was the resilience of their breeding activity in the face of environmental adversity. In times of scarcity entire populations of sparrows may have left for better parts, flying tens of kilometers from their usual haunts. Interrupted breeding may cause similar movements today, and the percentage of successful breeding attempts in new habitats is usually high. Unlike many other birds, house sparrows tend to persist in breeding after initial failures, and the early age at which they are capable of breeding provides a broad base of reproductive individuals in any given population.

In addition, the works of early agriculture often offered actual improvements from the point of view of the proto–house sparrows. One of the earliest inventions of farmers was irrigation, which served to provide a measure of stability in water supplies. This activity also enlarged the options of sparrows, who quickly mastered irrigation timetables to make use of the intermittent flow of artificially channeled water. The feces of domesticated herbivores, rich as they are in undigested food matter, soon provided a steady source of food for the new inquilines. In the centers of towns, where domestic animals might be protected from the depredations of nomadic human warriors, corrals became centers of sparrow activity and have continued to support vast populations of the birds to this day. Finally, as we have seen, the food of sparrows was identical to the food of humans. Inefficiencies in the processing of harvests, from field to kitchen table, have always provided ample opportunity for pilfering, and the role of house sparrows as scavengers and gleaners continues in modern cities much as it did in the days of Ur and Chaldea.

In retrospect, it seems almost as if the form and behavior of the original house sparrows already fit like a jigsaw puzzle piece into the new agricultural regime. Certainly, the worlds of the sparrow and the human have become one in the intervening millennia, and it is likely that the future courses of both species will be pretty much the same. We can likely rely on the proximity of house sparrows through all the coming centuries of humanity, and when the wilderness of forest and mountain have fallen to the axes and bulldozers of civilization, our urban wastes will continue to support thriving populations of these sturdy wildlings.

In this regard, the house sparrow is distinctly an asset. For all the damage done by the species, for all its cost (currently estimated at about fifty cents per bird per year in the United States), the house sparrow remains wild in our midst, a testament to the days of the lost Neolithic. Through its accessibility and numbers the species may serve as a teacher of biologic principle and law, joining other inquilines, such as house mice and Norway rats, in the researches of humanity.

Current trends suggest that Earth may yet reach a stage where it supports little beyond the constellation of plants and animals associated with human beings. In that sad time *Passer domesticus* and our other inquilines must be wilderness enough to awe the children of humankind's bittersweet triumph. Mark him well, the house sparrow. There's one outside your window this very minute.

2   The Starling

About 60 percent of all species of birds are classified in the order
Passeriformes along with the sparrows. They have radiated into
nearly every ecological niche available to land birds. Among the Oscines
alone, there are variations ranging from the hawklike shrike through the
seed-eating sparrow to the common starling, *Sturnus vulgaris,* whose omnivorous diet and aggressive behavior, manifested through an amazingly
intricate and coherent system of social exchange, have enabled it to share
so successfully the urban haunts of humankind. This is hardly surprising,
perhaps, when you consider the tendency of human cultures to reflect the
omnivorous diet, aggressive behavior, and amazingly intricate and coherent
system of social exchange characteristic of people. Civilization thus offers
the common starling a ready-made habitat, and it was not until the rise of
large towns that these birds took up with us so intimately. Starlings have
not associated with humans for as long as their distant cousins the house
sparrows have, but some of their habits have changed enough in conjunction with civilization to have fairly pinned them to the side of the
artificial system.

Sturnus vulgaris is a member of the family Sturnidae, which are
characteristically social omnivores, usually mainly black. They come in
sizes ranging from 17 to 45 centimeters in length, and sport a relatively
short tail and sharply pointed wings that form a distinctive triangular con-

figuration in flight. The true starlings include the mynas and glossy starlings of southeast Asia as well as our city cousins the common starlings. In their native ranges in Africa and Asia the several species of mynas occur as opportunist inquilines, and when the common myna was introduced to Australia, southern Africa, and certain Pacific islands, its adaptability and aggressiveness enabled it to sweep many native species from the scene and become a major destroyer of crops in some areas. Similarly, the crested myna has become an agricultural inquiline since its introduction to the Philippines, British Columbia, and the northwestern United States, and the congeneric Indian myna has taken over many niches formerly occupied by native birds since its introduction to the islands of Hawaii.

The Indian myna, an introduced inquiline in Hawaii, is little more than a large starling.

Most species of starlings possess a straight, sturdy beak. An interesting and emblematic behavioral trait of the family is the practice of inserting the closed beak into cracks in the ground or trees and then opening it forcibly to expose potential goodies such as insects. This habit is inborn and physically reflected by the structure of the skull and enlargement of the beak-opening muscles. In captivity the desire to pry in this manner is as strong as in the wild, and a tame starling will spend many hours inserting its beak between boards or the fingers or lips of human beings. This sort of uselessly persistent and automatic behavior is called vacuum activity by ethologists.

Starling pairs tend toward monogamy, and many remain bonded for years. Most nest in holes, several pairs often building nests in the same capacious hollows. Some construct communal nests reminiscent of those of weavers, although the common starling tends to build a single nest per pair and to defend this nest from other birds. Most starlings are not territorial beyond the entrance to the cup-shaped nest, and pairs jointly defend their nests from predation.

The common starling, our inquiline, hardly needs describing for urbanites of the western European tradition. Among flocks of blackbirds in the United States, starlings are the only short-tailed walkers one is likely to see. Twenty to twenty-two centimeters in length, adult starlings are mainly black overlaid with a magnificent iridescence of green, purple, and bronze. After the molt in late summer or early autumn, depending on the individual's age, the tips of the new feathers are white, giving winter starlings a speckled or streaked appearance. These tips wear off through the winter, and in the spring breeding season both male and female starlings are glossy black. During breeding season the beak of both sexes is bright yellow owing to the presence in the bloodstream of male hormones. This sexy bright beak fades to a dark brown as breeding ends, but even in winter the female may be identified by the pale base of her lower jaw. Eye color also differs between starling sexes. The iris of males is dull dark brown, that of females and juveniles paler and flecked with white at the rim in the manner of the "purty brown speckle eyes" beloved of the late author of the comic strip "Pogo." The newly fledged juvenile starling is gray-brown with a pale throat blending into white stripes at the top of the breast. The easily distinguished age, sex, and breeding status of starlings make them favorites of persons who study the social behavior of birds.

Before they entered the artificial system, common starlings raised a single brood of young annually and migrated to warmer lands in the winter. The arrival of the first farmers provided the birds with a new source of autumn and winter food, and many of them took shorter and shorter migratory flights in response to the new plenty. These innovative starlings avoided much of the tremendous expenditure of energy associated with migration, which is responsible for a large percentage of annual starling deaths; and because most of the migratory pattern is genetically inherited, such birds passed on their aberrant behavior to their young. The advantages gained by exploitation of our agricultural system have thus resulted in fixed alterations in the starling behavioral heritage.

Even today, however, some populations of starlings continue to migrate. Starlings along the Baltic Sea, for instance, migrate yearly to northwestern Germany to participate in the autumn harvests there, and lesser migrations still occur among central European starlings, whose annual trips to the Mediterranean and back are outstanding features of local natural history. The persistence of these habits shows that nonmigratory behavior is a relatively new occurrence among common starlings, and that the species as a whole is still undergoing a transition.

Interestingly, the genetic changes that ended migration among western European, British, and American starlings have not entirely eliminated the ghosts of the old behavior. The most sedentary Manhattan starling still experiences the ancient longing called *Zugunruhe* by the Germans, a twice-yearly night restlessness coinciding with the old autumn and spring migrations. The bird undergoing *Zugunruhe* repeatedly awakens and stirs about at night, fluttering from perch to perch and displaying all the neurotic agitation proper to one in need who knows not the object of his need.

The mechanism with which starlings locate feeding and wintering grounds, returning to the same breeding range each year, has for centuries amazed and mystified human observers. However, experiments subjecting captive birds to controlled sunlight conditions reveal that starlings experiencing *Zugunruhe* tend to orient themselves according to the position of the sun. When the apparent location of the sun is changed with mirrors, the birds orient themselves accordingly, and starlings subjected to an artificial day-night cycle show corresponding distortion in orientation when returned to the natural cycle. Other experiments suggest that the general direction of migration in any population of starlings may be inherited genetically. Young birds trapped during autumn migration and released some distance from their traditional path continue flying in the original direction regardless of changes in their ultimate destination, while adults of the same population tend to correct their routes and return to the traditional patterns. These experiments have incidentally established new wintering grounds for starling populations whose young participated in them; the displaced migrating juveniles returned year after year to their artificially induced destinations, and their descendants continue to do so to this day.

The first starlings to cease the long migratory flights of autumn and spring gained an additional advantage by their innovation. In the early spring, before the return of their vacationing cousins, they took possession of the better nesting sites, thus gaining some weeks in the breeding race. From single-brooded migratory ancestors these starlings founded a strain which was sedentary and capable of raising two broods per year. Instantly, the character of the species was changed. The new, more rapid reproductive rate permitted more efficient exploitation of the resources provided by agricultural efforts, and in a short time starlings changed from occasional consumers of agricultural products to true inquilines of European agricultural systems. The appearance of the nonmigratory starling appears to have taken place during medieval times, when much of northern and western Europe was put to the plow for the first time. By 1564 the new brand of sedentary starlings was so common that a British law was enacted offering rewards for starling heads. Such laws offered little protection against the growth of starling populations, however, and the success of the birds gradually became a liability as their numbers pressed toward the limits of available food and space. It was during these tight years that starlings for the first time began to exploit in great numbers the potential of the larger European cities.

It will be recalled that European cities of the Renaissance and before were filthy and disease-ridden places. Many main thoroughfares were equipped with great open sewers, into which all of the trash and waste of the metropolises found their way. Food supplies were inefficiently managed, and an abundance of organic matter of all sorts simply overflowed into the streets. Corpses, human and otherwise, ended up as often as not in the rivers around which most sizable cities of the time had grown, and in many places the criminal dead were displayed by the thousands on the gibbets and gallows of a grim justice. In short, cities became the end points for much of the energy and biomass distribution of the time, offering a new niche for animals catholic enough in taste and behavior to exploit it.

Common starlings were, and are, such animals. The new pressure of their numbers forced them to invade new places, and their social coherence and adaptability ultimately brought them to the cities. The major metropolitan avian inquiline at that time was the house sparrow, a smaller bird whose diet was largely vegetable, as we have seen. Because of their greater size, starlings did not compete directly with sparrows for nesting space. Furthermore, their all-inclusive diet permitted starlings to thrive in conjunction with the more specialized sparrows, and their superior strength and ferocity gave the newcomers an edge in any disport over resources that might arise between the two species. Ultimately a situation arose where sparrows and starlings shared the bounty of the cities in a state of perpetual mild animosity that has continued to this day.

Throughout most of its history, the common starling has been restricted in range to the western end of the Eurasian landmass. On the east, related species, such as the rose starling, *Sturnus rosea,* occupied most suitable habitats, while in Africa to the south both climate and native birds conspired to create an environment unsuitable to *S. vulgaris.* In the north it was simply too cold and lifeless, and to the west was the Atlantic Ocean, across which few land birds dare venture.

Humans, however, are inveterate crossers of oceans. With them they take small navigable bits of land called ships, and on ships, in the care of humans, starlings extended their range. The ecologically meddlesome British, as before, brought starlings to successful implantation in New Zealand in 1867, and the same British infested Australia with the birds so successfully that *S. vulgaris* was common on that continent by the turn of the century. The greatest transoceanic spread of starlings occurred in North America, where descendants of Europeans, profiting not at all from their experiences with house sparrows, repeatedly tried to inoculate the continent with starlings. The chief American exponent of starling importation was one Eugene Scheifflin, a wealthy drug manufacturer and guiding light of the American Acclimatization Society. Because of a perverted lust for the works of William Shakespeare, Scheifflin composed a list of every bird mentioned in the collected works of the Bard. He proposed to import and naturalize representatives of each such species, and to this demented end expended a considerable amount of cash and energy.

Prior to the materialization of the Scheifflin monomania, there had been several attempts to naturalize starlings for their supposedly beneficial insect-eating habits. From 1844 to 1890 starlings were imported from Europe by a variety of loopy, if well-meaning, and ecologically illiterate Europeans. Each of these attempts failed, perhaps because the new birds were installed in rural areas where native species already occupied potential starling ecological niches. Scheifflin, however, lived in New York City, from which most of the native avian population had already been extirpated. Shrewdly, the mad druggist chose for the location of his colony of imported birds that bit of Manhattan greenery still known as Central Park. On 6 March 1890, Scheifflin released forty pairs of starlings in Central Park and followed this introduction with the release of forty more birds on 25 April 1891. Along with the releases of starlings occurred those of other Shakespearian birds, none of which (luckily) survived.

Late in 1891 some twenty starlings appeared in Staten Island. By 1896 the birds were becoming a common sight in Brooklyn. Came the turn of the century, and *S. vulgaris* was already naturalized along most of the inhabited banks of the Hudson, down the east coast of New Jersey, and in Delaware and eastern Pennsylvania. Forty years later the species had spanned its adopted North America and was moving into Californian cities. For at least one Shakespearian bird, Scheifflin's dream had come true.

In the chapter on house sparrows, we examined some of the sensory systems responsible for their success and for that of birds in general. Starlings share with house sparrows the fantastic eyesight and orientation systems previously discussed; in addition, they are stronger fliers than sparrows and in many other ways are good subjects for a perusal of the bodily framework on which avian flight is built. As has been previously noted, the life of flying birds is dictated by the gaseous medium in which they move. All avian physical structures and systems are designed around the central fact of flight, and nowhere is this centrality more visibly demonstrated than in the construction of the skeletal and muscular systems. These systems are remarkably similar from order to order of birds, the starling being bone for bone nearly identical to the eagle or the duck or the penguin. Even between species as diverse as the huge flightless ostrich and the tiny hummingbird, there is nowhere near as much skeletal diversity as is found among mammalian orders such as primates, carnivores, and cetaceans. A single starling is an eloquent testament to the triumph of archosaurian engineering over the stresses of a flying existence.

The systems responsible for processing the foodstuffs which fuel this extraordinary flying machine are every bit as remarkable as the frame itself. Because of the tremendously high metabolic rate of the bird, food must be constantly and rapidly processed in order to provide sufficient energy for operation of the flying system, and to this end the starling digestive system is a marvel of efficiency in form and function.

The beak is the chief manipulative organ of the starling. From nest-building to exposure, dismemberment, and carrying of food, the beak serves as a ready and adaptable tool for interaction with the environment. Because of the starling's preference for meat, much of it alive and wriggling, the palate is provided with sharp, backward-pointing papillae, which pierce the prey and help prevent its escape. However, the starling cannot chew, for like other birds, it has discarded teeth in its long evolutionary quest for lightness. The mouth is provided with mucous glands with which the bird softens and lubricates the large bites of food necessitated by a toothless existence, and salivary glands, present only in the throat, break down any starchy content in the food and lubricate it as it slides down the short esophagus. Although poorly equipped with organs of taste in comparison with mammals of similar size, the starling's mouth is very sensitive to touch.

The esophagus is a short tube, also lined with lubricating mucous glands, serving to conduct food from the mouth to the crop, which is simply an enlargement of the esophagus, a storage bin in which the starling can store a large quantity of hastily eaten food. This capability for storage permits birds to eat large amounts of food at once, an adaptation permitting minimal exposure to terrestrial predators at mealtime. In the starling the crop takes the form of a bag resting in the curve of the wish-

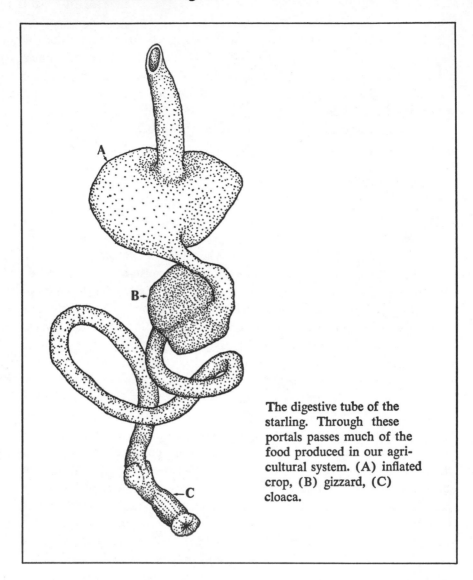

The digestive tube of the starling. Through these portals passes much of the food produced in our agricultural system. (A) inflated crop, (B) gizzard, (C) cloaca.

bone, small when empty but visibly changing the shape of the bird when full. Although no real digestion appears to take place there, the crop is lined with more mucous glands, which continue the softening of stored food. In addition, the crop is lined with a tough epithelium designed to protect its walls from the chemical defenses of poisonous insects, of which the starling may happily consume vast quantities at a sitting.

The avian stomach is a two-part affair functioning both as the usual vertebrate stomach and as a set of chewing jaws for its toothless possessor.

Food passing from the crop first enters the proventriculus, or glandular stomach, in which digestive enzymes are secreted. This stomach is an archosaurian innovation, not found in reptiles or mammals, preparing the food for the grinding and crushing that takes place in the muscular stomach or gizzard. This organ consists of a sac enclosed by two massive lenses of muscle, which in the starling may exert a combined crushing strength of more than 100 kilograms. The gizzard is lined with glands that secrete a layer of hard ridges and plates, between which the shells of insects and other hard foods are easily crushed to a pulp. Birds may occasionally swallow a few pebbles to increase the grinding surface, and some larger extinct terrestrial archosaurians swallowed several kilograms of stony grit (called gastroliths, "bellystones," by paleontologists), which survive to this day among their fossilized ribs.

Having passed through the gizzard, the starling's meal is now a mush of food and digestive juices. Beyond the gizzard is the intestine, in which the most intensive digestion and absorption of nutrients take place. Unlike that of mammals, the avian intestine is not divided into distinct regions but is composed of a simple tube coiled in the body cavity between the gizzard and anus. In birds whose main diet is meat, the intestine is relatively short, in keeping with the easy digestibility and high food value per volume characteristic of animal food. In those with a diet of hard seeds and the like, such as sparrows, the intestine must be long enough to extract the most nutriment possible from the necessarily larger quantities of such food that must be eaten to fuel the seed-eater. In the omnivorous starling the intestine is of the medium length (about 12 centimeters), suitable to one who may eat almost anything at all. Through the walls of this tube the bird assimilates almost all of its food, until the tiny remaining amount reaches the saclike caeca near the end. These masses of lymphatic tissue are believed to absorb excess water and digested proteins from the food mass, and any matter remaining composes the small dark moist portion of the starling droppings so often seen on the windshields of automobiles and the pediments of buildings.

At the posterior end of the intestine lies the cloaca, or "sewer," an enlargement of the tube divided into three distinct regions. The first part of the cloaca reached by food on its journey through the starling is called the coprodaeum. Receiving the dark mass passed by the bird's caeca, the coprodaeum stores this remnant until enough is accumulated to pass on to the next region, the urodaeum, into which the kidneys and genital organs empty their products. The discharge from the kidneys, unlike that of most mammals, contains little water. Most of a starling's water is used in the bird's cooling system, and bird urine is usually a white, chalky paste of uric acid and a few other unusable products of metabolism. Combined with the remaining intestinal waste, this urine finally passes into the proctodaeum, the last segment of the cloaca, which is terminated by the sphincter muscle of the anus. Equipped with a set of powerful squeezing muscles, the proctodaeum ejects feces and urine a considerable distance, keeping the immediate roosting or nesting surface clear of droppings and showering them instead on human citizens below. Associated with the proctodaeum in young starlings is a glandular lump called the bursa Favricius, part of the antibody-response system preventing infection from food. In adult birds this pocket loses its function and atrophies until it is nearly invisible.

Two important glands associated with digestion are the pancreas and the liver. In starlings the pancreas is large and important in the production of digestive enzymes. Like the pancreas in mammals, the avian pancreas is responsible for the synthesis of certain enzymes involved in the assimilation of sugars, most notably insulin. The liver is the largest gland in the starling's body, rather larger even than the liver of mammals of comparable mass. The avian liver, like the mammalian liver, is a storer of fats and sugars, a synthesizer of proteins, and an excretor of waste from the metabolic system. Bile, the bitter green liquid stored in the gall bladder, is also secreted by the liver. This compound aids in the breakdown of fatty matter in the bird's diet, entering the intestine just posterior to the gizzard. The liver serves as a neutralizer of poisons, to the dismay of those who would control the starling population by poisoning; a starling may withstand nearly a thousand times the amount of some poisonous plant alkaloids that would drop a human adult, a testament to the superb miniaturized chemical plant that is the avian liver.

A starling may consume a quarter of its own mass in food in a day, equivalent to the author's consuming some 18 kilograms (about 40 pounds) of food during each twenty-four-hour period, day in and day out! Because of its tremendous energy requirements, however, the starling does not exhibit the change in mass that would surely accompany such trenchermanship in humans. The prodigious avian appetite is controlled, as in mammals, by an area of the brain called the hypothalamus, which may be experimentally stimulated to alter the bird's eating habits. If a "hunger site" in the hypothalamus is stimulated by means of a tiny electrode implanted in the bird's brain, he will eat beyond satiation until his crop ruptures and he dies; conversely, if the "satiation centers" are stimulated, the animal will starve in full sight of good food, being under the impression that he is full and well.

The starling shares with humans a diet known as euryphagous; it eats almost anything at all. Being a bird, however, the starling must eat foods that are rich in energy relative to their masses. When he can, the starling chooses animal food or rich fruits rather than grasses, foliage, or wood. The starlings' love of rich foods often results in their cooperative monopolizing of suet stands at bird feeders, an example of their coordinated social feeding habits. Starling eating patterns are organized around communal behavior, the birds feeding heavily *en masse* during the cool of the morning and foraging in smaller flocks throughout the rest of the day. Groups of starlings are known to cooperate in the killing of larger prey, some even attacking small vertebrates such as mice when there are enough of the birds to get the drop on them. In the evening, flocks of full starlings return to roost, where they spend the night in digestion, and they meet the next morning both well supplied with energy and—again—hungry. In addition, starlings and other birds drink large quantities of water, necessary to maintain healthy temperature levels under conditions of maximal physical activity. On a warm day a starling may lose some 40 percent of its body water through its evaporative cooling system, and this lost water must constantly be replaced. Flocks of the birds visit traditional watering places where possible, often chasing other birds away and monopolizing the water supply.

While individual starlings are less than cerebral dynamos, starling populations are surprisingly adaptable entities, more than able to circumvent the hostile machinations of their human landlords. The sum of experience of hundreds of starlings makes up the "brain" of the flock, its nerve impulses being the calls of each bird. Because of the unpredictable ways of human beings, starling populations are constantly forced to revise their learning, to catch up on each change in the artificial ecosystem. In response to a situation known only to itself, a new source of food perhaps, one starling speaks, and the flock acts. The resulting constant revision and accumulation of flock experience has produced not only a supremely adaptable inquiline but a vocally accomplished one indeed.

The language of starlings is among the most complex and to the point among animals. Unlike the taught-learned linguistic system of humans, the starling language is built on a framework of inherited calls and other displays common to all members of the species *S. vulgaris.* However, when starlings invade new habitats (as they always do, given a chance), their call system experiences a "linguistic drift," with different populations speaking in increasingly different dialects as time goes on. Such drift comes with imperfect *learning* and direct *innovation,* both elements characteristic of the evolution of human languages, or, indeed, any sophisticated information exchange system—including that which is life itself.

Starling flocks express a wide variety of environmental conditions with their voices. Commonly, one starling will sight a potential predator and speak of it to his fellows with the following precision:

A Dog.

A Human, unarmed.

A Cat (or other mammal predatory on starlings).

A Hawk or *An Owl* (predatory only on mammals).

A Falcon (predatory on starlings).

Or, most important, *A Human, armed!*

Threat stance of starling, a form of "speech" using the feathers, with which the bird attempts to appear larger and more ferocious.

Each of these contingencies necessitates a different flock response; thus each must be clearly articulated in a manner suitable to the size and hearing range of the flock. The advent of new predation-type situations, such as janitors and traps, requires the modification of the vocabulary of a given population to prevent its extinction, and in this way starling "language" evolves. Interestingly, the predator-alarm calls of many avian species, including starlings, are markedly similar, permitting a number of species to benefit from one bird's experience. Most familiar of such calls are the *chink* noises used to announce the presence of a terrestrial predator; the easily located originator of the sound permits other birds to locate the predator and, perhaps, mob it and run it off. On the other hand, a small bird spotting a falcon on the wing utters a high-pitched *seeet* noise that is not easily located by the winged predator but that adequately transmits the bad news to other potential prey species.

With its voice an individual starling not only communicates the location and nature of predators, but also identifies himself to other individuals, announces his sex and breeding condition, defends nest and position in the flock's pecking order, locates and attracts a mate, calls other individual starlings, musters the flock, ends or begins the roost, announces the nature and whereabouts of food, and expresses his current emotional state. Because of the strong imitative streak inherent in starling behavior, young birds are quick to pick up on the flock dialect and integrate themselves with the group.

With such an elaborate system of verbal communication, the starling requires a complex and responsive vocal system. Its chief sound-producing organ, the syrinx, is a structure found nowhere but among archosaurians, and in animals possessing the syrinx there are no vocal cords as in mammals. The syrinx is composed of a boxlike enlargement of the trachea at the point where the bronchial tubes separate on their ways to the lungs. The cartilaginous and flexible tracheae, composed of rings of cartilage, are at this point surrounded by muscles that vary the volume of the syrinx according to what is being said. Inside the box are two sets of thin mem-

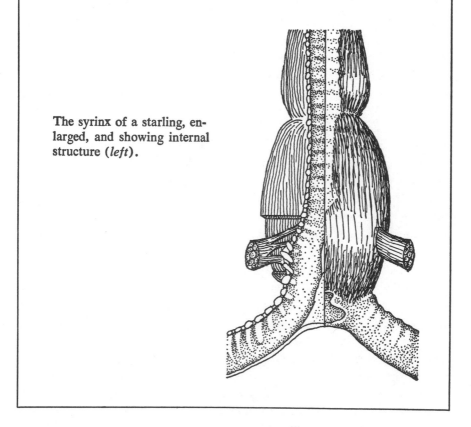

The syrinx of a starling, enlarged, and showing internal structure (*left*).

branes through which the passage of air is modulated, producing the exquisite voice control characteristic of starlings and many other oscine birds, as well as such famous vocalists as parrots.

Corresponding to the starling's vocal apparatus is its highly developed sense of hearing. The auditory system in reptiles, mammals, and archosaurians is largely similar, having been perfected at an early date in the evolution of terrestrial vertebrates. Hearing begins at the outside of the starling's skull, where the two external ear openings are hidden by feathers. When cocking its head to hear more acutely, the starling may erect these feathers to funnel more sound to the openings, thus changing its head shape and adopting a characteristic "listening" attitude. The distance between the external ear openings is large enough for the bird to detect differences in soundwave phase at each opening, thus permitting triangulation and precise location of such noisemakers as insects.

The starling ear can "resolve" separate sounds spaced as little as six ten-thousandths of a second apart, and the song of starlings and many other oscine birds, while far more complex than can be detected by the human ear, packs a great deal of information understandable to these birds into small spaces of time. All of this speaking and listening on the part of starlings reflects their most significant adaptation and the secret of their sudden success in the human context, the institutions of communal roosting and feeding. Groups of more than a million starlings may return each evening to a traditional roosting place, great clouds of the birds following established routes from daytime feeding grounds up to 60 kilometers away. The communal roost serves a number of purposes advantageous to its members. Perhaps most obvious of these is the protection from predation offered by so vast a number of starlings, each equipped with sharp eyes and ears, squashed into a small and usually protected situation. Even in flight, starlings compress their formations whenever a falcon appears, and often a starling flock turns the tables by attacking a flying predator *en masse*.

In Europe, some starling roosts have been used for centuries, often profoundly altering conditions in areas surrounding the roost site. The droppings from so many starlings kills plants and drives other animals away, and oxygen consumption by birds packed as close as forty per cubic meter causes a profound if temporary alteration in the local air composition. Furthermore, air temperature may be modified by such congregations; roosts respond to temperature changes by altering their spacing. Normally, starlings roost just out of pinching distance one from another, but in extremely cold weather the animals huddle for warmth. A lone starling in a

Normal spacing of roosting starlings (*above*) and huddling in cold weather (*below*).

cold evening must consume a great deal of oxygen in order to maintain body heat, but huddled starlings may reduce individual oxygen consumption by a factor of nine or ten through their proximity to one another.

Communal roost sites may change in response to environmental pressures. Rural roosts tend to gravitate toward urban areas when autumn begins to reduce the food supply in the country. Cities metabolize approximately the same amount of resources throughout the year, and their winter food waste may be the primary diet for large populations of starlings. Thus it is in the autumn and winter that starling roosts seem most often to cross their human landlords and it is during these times of the year that such roosts incur the massive shooting and poisoning and other agonistic behavior characteristic of humans on whose possessions is rained starling crap.

The closely social habits of the starling do have distinct disadvantages. As we know all too well, dense aggregations of human beings permit conditions in which parasites thrive and wastes accumulate. Starlings are similarly affected by crowding, being so highly susceptible to infestations of disease that they serve as immense reservoirs for various avian parasites. Because other birds, such as grackles, cowbirds, redwinged blackbirds, robins, and sparrows, join the vast feeding flocks of starlings, the latter are likely to become infected with a wider variety of diseases than if their flocks were composed only of starlings. Furthermore, the euryphagous diet of starlings exposes them to disorders which they might otherwise never have encountered. Such diseases of mammals as viral enteritis are passed from feedlot to feedlot by starlings that eat the feces of infected animals and pass the virus on through their own droppings. *Histoplasma capsulatum,* a fungus parasitic on warm-blooded vertebrates, is also transmitted through starlings, and some half-million American humans are thus exposed to the fungus yearly, about twenty-five thousand of these developing the feverish anemia characteristic of histoplasmosis.

Strictly among themselves, starlings maintain an impressive collection of parasites. Externally, a population of the birds may harbor more than twenty species of ticks and mites alone, not to mention the many lice and other arthropods that have evolved to exploit a habitat of feathers. About ninety species of internal parasites have been identified in American and European starlings, only eleven of these parasites being shared between the hemispheres. Such parasite diversity reflects the wide variety of environments exploited by starlings, exposing them to far more potential parasites than more specialized birds might ever hope to meet. In short, the many diseases present in starling populations are actually a function of their tremendous success—like the diseases of humans, one of the prices paid for social triumph.

Their very exposure to disease, however, has produced in starling populations a vitality rarely approached by other animals. Centuries of rigorous selection have resulted in starlings that are so resistant to disease as to be able to invade new biomes and encounter new diseases with marked success.

As we have seen, a multitude of starlings exhibits the combined learning of all its individual members. Because starlings are rather more endowed with learning capability than most birds, such a multitude is usually quickly able to discover and evade the slings and arrows of outraged humanity. Starling aptitude has been tested by human rage throughout the centuries during which they have shared our harvests. With an estimated cost to the American economy of eighty-four cents per starling (wouldn't you love to find out how these bureaucrats arrive at such figures?), the birds eat a sizable chunk out of farm profits and city maintenance funds. More recently, with the advent of powered human flight, starlings have posed a new problem around airports. With their cleared land and often suburban siting, airports become breeding and grazing places for large numbers of insects and thus places of meeting for hundreds of thousands of starlings—any one of which, sucked into the intake of a jet engine, may cause the wreck of an airplane. It is perhaps at the ends of runways that the severest tests of starling adaptability occur, with great pressure being exerted on airport starling populations by the administrators of said ports. It may ultimately transpire that airports can be rid of starlings only by making the runways unattractive to insects—and places unattractive to these most successful of all land animals are mighty hard to find.

Because of the massive damage caused by aggregations of hundreds of thousands of ravening or defecating starlings, humans have invented dozens of novel and largely ineffective ways to eliminate them. Fake hawks and humans ("scarestarlings"), guns, mortars, nets and other traps, poisons, detergents to eliminate the waterproofing quality of feathers, sticky goo to repel perchers, electrified wire, spotlights powered by little motors, shiny metal blowing in the wind, all result simply in alteration of starling behavior to circumvent them. When recorded starling distress calls were broadcast at roosting flocks from public address speakers, the birds were properly agitated—for a time—until they discovered the speakers themselves, which in some cases they attacked! All this is hardly surprising, though, for the starling's very finest specialization is its ability to coexist with and frustrate the designs of its landlords.

For all the disagreeable consequences of their behavior, starlings do perform some economically useful tasks. It has been discovered that starlings are a vector of the milky white fungus which is a parasite of the soil-breeding and highly injurious Japanese beetle, *Popillia japonica*. Infected grubs of these beetles may be exhumed and eaten by starlings, and spores of the fungus pass unharmed through the bird's digestive tract and out with the feces. These spores remain dormant wherever they fall, until they happen to encounter more Japanese beetle grubs, which they infect as before. Intentionally infected soil in areas where starlings feed has resulted in a significant decrease in the local Japanese beetle population, even though the starlings consume relatively few of the larvae themselves. More directly, starlings may be found wherever insects congregate (as at airports), and more than one farmer has been saved by the descent of a horde of starlings on invasions of locusts or other pests. During the breeding season, more than four-fifths of a starling nestling's diet may consist of insects injurious to agriculture, and starlings with young are little more than animated insect traps during the daylight hours. Aggregations of starlings also sometimes serve to increase local populations of raptorial birds such as falcons, hawks, and owls, whose presence is an asset to any community. In a few cases the large accumulations of starling guano around traditional roosts have been used successfully as guano for fertilizer. Finally, starlings may be eaten by humans. In Italy thousands of the birds are marketed as a delicacy yearly, and the author himself has eaten them and found them delicious—better in taste, in fact, than most of the popular gallinaceous game birds such as pheasants and grouse. If the eating of starlings were popularized, it is likely that many of the problems caused by the press of starling numbers might quickly be alleviated. Four-and-twenty blackbirds baked in a pie is a good meat course for about eight adult humans, and there is no closed season on starlings.

Then again, on an individual basis the starling can be a very attractive, even endearing, animal. The adaptability that has enabled starlings to succeed so well against our wishes is the result of a learning apparatus more capable than that of most birds. The starling can even be said to be a smart bird, as birds go, and its intelligence is reflected in behavior that sometimes seems to be comically anthropomorphic. This is particularly true in cases where infant starlings are raised by human beings; such tamed birds characteristically participate in the human household with vigor and flair. Indeed, unlike the house sparrow, the starling makes an ideal pet for those who enjoy the company of birds; it is free for the taking, being unprotected by law, and its sturdiness and omnivorous diet make it easily cared for in the unnatural surroundings of a human home. In addition, starlings share the imitative behavior common to the family Sturnidae; like their cousins the mynas, starlings may learn to repeat phrases of human language with astonishing accuracy, often minutely imitating the voices of individual humans. Finally, because of the elaborate social structures of which starlings are naturally a part, tame specimens tend to blend well into small human societies such as families, often treating their hosts like other starlings on a basis of complete and sometimes disconcerting equality. The relatively long life of a well-cared-for pet starling, about twenty years, offers years of amusing interspecific relations on the personal level.

So ends this quick glance at our little cousin the common starling, uncommonly good at what he does. We see him as accomplished thief, stealing from us with an irritating flamboyance all out of proportion to his size. We see him as behaviorally gaudy and arrogant, a noisy blusterer supremely confident in the strength of his numbers. We see him as a dirty crapper, raining tons of guano on our cities and farmlands. Yet the starling also represents life at its loving best. As a world citizen, he shares with us the pinnacle of vertebrate evolution. In many ways our behavioral patterns are similar, as befits two such opportunistic species traveling the same path. In the end, surely, *S. vulgaris* is deserving of at least a grudging respect on our part. And so, grudgingly, I salute the starling.

3 The Pigeon

Of all our vertebrate inquilines, the rock dove, *Columba livia,* native of the mountains of Eurasia and northern Africa, has been most intensely altered by its long proximity with us. In addition to a long and prosperous inquilinism dating from the Neolithic of the Near East, rock doves have undergone the uniquely cultural mutualism called domestication. In this symbiosis we have altered and molded the genetic structure of the rock dove through purposeful selection over a period of more than five thousand years, producing pigeons that in most cases would never survive a return to the native habitat. However, the cities and towns of agricultural humanity remain haven for these artificial birds, providing airspace entirely devoid of falcons, and feeding grounds that have seen neither snake nor fox for centuries. In these safe places the beautifully twisted mutant pigeons pool their genes to produce an echo of the wild ancestor—the city rock dove whose entire existence is supported by human love. It is the affection for pigeons among the sons and daughters of men, manifested as it is in pigeon-feeding in the park, that assures the continued success of the rock dove as an inquiline of the artificial system. In the face of mounting evidence that city pigeons are vectors of many human diseases and are major pollutants in urban areas, their numbers continue to rise as more and more humans simply feed them, watching their activity with a uniquely human pleasure.

And they *are* a pleasure to behold, these murmuring iridescent ghostly gray things. Even when the first towns appeared, containing the homes of prosperous fishing and grass-growing peoples, rock doves occasionally descended from the sheer cliffs on which they nested to share the bounty of Neolithica. The first Middle Eastern towns to survive the depredations of neighboring tribes for a few hundred years probably attracted nesting rock doves, and in due time human beings discovered the squab, the fledgling rock dove, most delicious of fowls.

With the eating of squabs came a change in the ecological status of rock doves. From incidental nesters in the homes and temples of early towns, the birds became welcome guests, for whom space was enthusiastically prepared. With the first building of artificial nesting holes for rock doves, the art of dovecote culture was born and humanity was on its way to what was probably the first domestication of a bird.

Originally there was no selection by humans for specific characteristics, but early perfection of the dovecote resulted in a mutualism that was to cause the first artificial changes in the structure of rock dove populations. The nesting boxes provided by early dove enthusiasts were often built right into the walls of houses and other buildings. These boxes were open at both ends, and a limited amount of nesting space was available for each pair of doves. If several young were present in a single box, the smallest of them tended to be pushed through the inner end of the box into a trough from which it could be retrieved for breakfast by the maintainer of the dovecote. In this manner larger and larger pigeons were selected as generations of the birds took to breeding in dovecotes. Otherwise, they remained essentially wild, self-feeding and self-watering, free to come and go as they pleased. After all these thousands of years the dovecote remains one of the niftiest automatic meat-producing machines known to humanity.

This cheerful and purposeful relationship probably continued for thousands of years before the first artificial breeding of pigeons began. By 4500 B.C. extensive pigeon dinners were being served at parties in Mesopotamia, reflecting an already efficient and productive dovecote culture. Ruins of buildings elaborately equipped with ledges and holes for rock doves are still plentiful throughout the Near East and northern Africa

During these early centuries other pigeons came with the rock dove to share the advantages of dovecote culture—reduced predation, plentiful food, mor than adequate shelter and nesting conditions. Occasional inquilinist c relatives of the rock dove include the stock dove, *Columba*

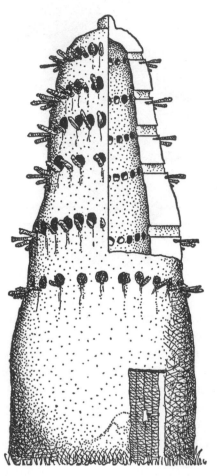

An Egyptian dovecote, show-ing cross section of nesting holes and interior. These structures are still built as they have been for five thousand years.

oenas, the turtledove, *Streptopelia turtur,* and the collared dove, *S. decaoto,* all of which still inhabit cities of Europe and Asia. The Barbary dove, *S. risoria,* was another of these early sharers of the human environment, and these have been domesticated to a certain extent. Even today, certain wild doves show a tendency to move into agricultural towns to participate in the harvest, the Inca dove, *Scardafella inca,* of the Americas being a famous example.

But it was ultimately the rock dove that was to dominate the place of order Columbiformes among humans. Named after its most familiar

The dodo, *Raphus cucullus,* a giant flightless pigeon.

members, as most of these orders are, the Columbiformes include, in addition to the true pigeons and doves, the aberrant family Pteroclididae, the sand grouse, terrestrial pigeons that have converged in form and behavior with true grouse. Also classed among the Columbiformes are the extinct dodos of family Raphidae, giant flightless pigeons that are known only from the Mascarene Islands east of Madagascar, to which some flock of pigeons was blown millions of years ago. Untroubled by mammals and other terrestrial predators, these fruit-eaters reached the size and mass of turkeys as they lost the ability to fly through millennia of island life. The advent of European humans with their assortment of pigs, cats, dogs, and rats ended the race of dodos within decades, the last of the big birds having died more than two centuries ago. Interestingly, the presence of the dodo on the isolated Mascarenes permitted the distribution of the fruit of a large tree, *Calvaria major,* which coevolved with the dodo to such an extent that its seeds would not germinate unless they were first eaten by a dodo. The mighty gizzard of the dodo apparently digested an impervious covering from these seeds, permitting moisture to reach the plant germ within. The trees attracted dodos by coating these seeds in a tasty fruit on which dodos doted, and with the extinction of the dodos came the end of natural distribution of *Calvaria major.* By 1973 there were only thirteen of the trees left in the Mascarenes, the rest having been killed for

lumber in the centuries since the extinction of dodos. Although seeds of
C. major have been found among the bones of dodos, it was not until a
modern experimenter force-fed turkeys with fresh ripe fruits that these
seeds could be induced to germinate. The successful outcome of these
experiments may have resulted in the first new *C. major* to have germinated
since the late seventeenth century.

Leaving the poor old dodos, we return to family Columbidae, the true
pigeons and doves, which constitute the majority of the order Columbiformes. These 255 species, in about 43 genera, share a generally stout
build, short legs, and a weak bill provided with a cere, a waxy bare area
about the nostrils. Pigeons are generally considered to be about midway
up (or down) the avian evolutionary ladder, distantly related to the
tropical and subtropical parrots of order Psittaciformes, with whom they
share a largely vegetarian diet of fruits and seeds. In addition, the true
pigeons and doves produce "pigeon's milk," a unique substance produced
by the epithelial wall of the crop for the nourishment of very young squabs
and resembling rabbit's milk in composition. This milk is necessary to provide sufficient protein and fat during the rapid growth of infancy, for
these vegetarian birds do not alter their parental feeding pattern to collect
insects and other high-protein food for the young.

In general, pigeons and doves show a fairly small degree of sexual
dimorphism, since they are nonterritorial colonial nesters and therefore
have not evolved the secondary sexual characteristics, such as brightly
colored male plummage, that are mainly products of territorial competition.
The male may be slightly larger and more massive than the female, but
the sexes share the same color scheme in most cases and there is little
behavioral difference between them. Indeed, the male pigeon produces
milk right along with the female and is quite as intimately involved in
rearing the young. Most members of family Columbidae are flashy-colored,
tropical, fruit-eating pigeons, but the rock doves and other temperate
columbids are generally quiet-colored birds ranging from the muted grays
and blacks of the wild rock dove through the soft browns and beiges of
the wild North American doves and pigeons. All Columbidae are monoga-
mous, with the female building a simple cup-shaped nest from materials
brought by the male. In some cases, such as that of our cliff-dwelling rock
dove, the building of nests has been reduced to the rough lining of a
scrape or depression on a suitable ledge.

Unlike the intelligent, vociferous starling and the raucously aggressive
house sparrow, rock doves and their relatives are fairly quiet birds. Suffered
as inquilines because of their attractiveness and food value to humans, rock

doves have less need of intelligence and adaptability than do the other birds that have taken to living in cities. Consequently, the behavior of rock doves seems rather rigid and socially simple. This simplicity of behavior stems from the fact that pigeons are almost entirely herbivorous and have never required the complex behavioral attributes needed to outwit and prey on insects and other animals. Further, until recently the rock dove has enjoyed the active protection of humans rather than their enmity and thus has never evolved the strategies utilized by such inquilines as starlings and sparrows in their centuries-old battle with the human landlord.

Although rock doves probably coexisted with humans for several millennia before true domestication began, it is not until the Fifth Dynasty of Egypt, five thousand years ago, that we find the first evidence for intentional selection of certain characteristics in the birds. It is not precisely clear what the ancient Egyptians wanted from their rock doves, but records of purchases and stud sheets from that remote era have survived, indicating that a complex and structured breeding program had already begun the process of physical differentiation that was to result in the many modern races of domestic rock doves. Early pigeon breeders seem to have concentrated their efforts on isolating certain peculiarities of color and feather structure, but variation in homing ability was quickly recognized. By 1198 B.C. the Egyptians had perfected the breeding of homing pigeons to such an extent that in that year the pharaoh Ramses III marked his coronation with a release of homing pigeons to the four directions.

Pigeon breeding became common around the Mediterranean in the first millennium B.C. and domestic rock doves assumed a religious significance to the Hebrews, who sacrificed thousands of the birds annually in their temples. The first white dove is recorded from Greece in 478 B.C. and domestic doves spread rapidly in trade with the Far East and the western shores of Europe. The early Romans adopted dovecote culture (as so much else!) from the Egyptians and Greeks, early recognizing the communications potential embodied in the homing ability of their new wards. Generals released pigeons in the field to bring news of victory to Rome, and the outcome of the infamous games was announced to rural, gladiator-breeding patricians by agents who released homing pigeons in the Circus.

The Romans spread dovecote culture across civilized Europe, introducing rock doves to the British Isles and much of northern and central Europe. The prior presence of towns enabled many escapees from Roman dovecotes to establish wild inquiline populations in new areas, where they were protected as usual by their human landlords. However, with the decline of Roman influence the use of pigeons for communications seems to have largely disappeared in Europe. Squabs were still eaten by the nobles of the time, though, and most great houses possessed a few dovecotes, whose inhabitants were permitted by law to forage in the fields of the serfs. Things being as they were, serfs were prevented from resisting the depredations of m'lord's doves; these birds therefore added to m'lord's annual take of grain from his serfs, helping to make the feudal system a great success with the wellborn.

During the medieval centuries it was the Arabs who maintained the finest and most elaborate genealogies of rock doves, developing the art of raising homing pigeons to new heights. In the Nation of Islam the pigeon became an object of reverence, then a necessity as the outposts of that far-flung empire were tied together in a homing-pigeon telegraph net. This process culminated in the establishment, in A.D. 1150, of a permanent pigeon post by the sultan of Baghdad.

Carried to India, dovecote culture and the breeding of homing pigeons helped advance the cause of Islam at the expense of more ancient civilizations, and the Indians came to revere the rock dove, as they do to the present day. Ultimately Genghis Khan employed a pigeon communications system to integrate the strategies of his Mongol buddies, and through him the rock dove may have helped to alter the genetic constitution and history of many of the peoples of eastern Europe who were subject to the activity of Genghis's merry men.

With the European Renaissance came a new interest among Westerners in the art of dovecote culture and its corollary, the breeding of homing pigeons. Improving on the work of Arabs and Far Easterners, Europeans established new bloodlines and maintained proven ones, to the general advantage of the homing breeds. The people of Belgium, living as they do on real estate whose ownership has been hotly contested for millennia, seem to have perfected the homing pigeon for military communications purposes. More than a century ago in Belgium the first Carrier pigeons were isolated and bred from older homing stock, and with them was born the modern sport of pigeon racing.

Throughout the world the perpetual military conflict and territorial adventurousness of European civilization produced a need for efficient communication never before seen on earth. The Carrier pigeon and its derivatives were adopted by military systems across the globe, and intensely competitive breeding on many continents quickly produced new and better homing breeds. International prizes were offered for pigeons flying the farthest, fastest, and most accurately to their home bases, and such institutions as the U.S. Army Signal Corps became innovators in the production of truly masterful homing pigeons. A Signal Corps pigeon, Smoky Girl, was the first to take a prize offered for a bird that could fly 500 miles safely and accurately; after repeating the feat three times in rapid succession, this bird was set to breeding, and her descendants number among the thousands in racing breeds today. The "opening" of the American West to the depredations of Europeans was made possible partly by homing pigeons, immune as they were to the desperate attempts by the American aboriginals to cut communications lines and save a bit of their homeland from the invaders. While an Amerindian might cut a telegraph line or dislodge some railroad ties, he had little chance of stopping a message carried by pigeon to array the forces of European technology against him. Thus the Europeans profited from the experiences of Genghis Khan in the use of pigeons as a tool for conquest.

Today the racing pigeon continues to make itself useful in communications. In Japan and other places where electronic communications systems may be interrupted by earthquake, newspapers still maintain dovecotes for the purpose of transporting scoops to city rooms, and in China the early triumphs of Mao Tse-tung Thought were carried across that mighty nation on the legs of pigeons. In many mountainous parts of American Formosa and other such places, cattle semen is flown to remote points for breeding purposes by pigeons, whose speed assures the live transmission of prize spermatozoa. Today in the United States and western Europe, private pigeon-racing enthusiasts number among the tens of thousands, most supporting one or two pairs of birds, which they release at weekend races. Each racer in the United States is banded, and the number of each band, together with the name and address of the wearer's owner, is recorded by the American Racing Pigeon Association. Modern racing pigeons routinely make flights of up to 3800 kilometers, at speeds averaging 80 to 90 kilometers per hour, and occasionally such spirited birds get lost. With prices ranging into the hundreds of dollars for good racers, and into the tens of thousands for birds of champion stock, banded racers represent considerable investments to their owners and should, of course, be returned as soon as possible if found. Such returns sometimes establish striking records for length of flight; a pigeon lost near Los Angeles finally turned up in the Canal Zone of Panama!

The exact workings of the homing process are still uncertain in terms of scientific research. Since birds first took to the air they have needed a strong sense of orientation. Because pigeons feed in areas that are often many kilometers away from their nesting sites, a strong sense of direction must have appeared early in the evolution of the pigeon family. With the advent of dovecote culture, humans often noticed distinctive birds far from their roosts. Curiosity about the birds' mode of getting about probably sparked the first Egyptian experiments with homing, and it was early established that homing had both innate and learned elements. A bird that distinguished itself with some feat of homing might be allowed to breed under controlled conditions; such birds usually transmitted some of their ability to their young, and thousands of generations of selection for homing have resulted in birds that are far ahead of wild rock doves in homing ability. However, the fact remains that pigeons must learn to home properly and that even young birds of the finest and most advanced homing stock must undergo periods of rigorous training before they are set free to seek their home dovecotes.

Modern experimentation suggests that pigeons released up to 16 or 20 kilometers from home rely on landmarks to locate their dovecotes. Beyond 16 to 20 kilometers, and perhaps to 80 kilometers, such birds may show disorientation for a time, spiraling about a bit before striking out directly for the home point. Around 80 kilometers from home another system takes over, in which the bird immediately orients itself toward home and takes off. It is currently believed that at distances beyond 80 kilometers homing pigeons refer to a "biocoordinate grid system" based on two or more parameters made available to the birds through sensory systems yet imperfectly understood. For instance, when distances become great enough to affect a postulated system of magnetic orientation, pigeons may correlate this magnetic coordinate with another parameter, possibly the position of the sun, to establish cross references on the path home. The exact mechanism behind feats of homing remains a mystery, though, and to complicate the matter it has been established that, except in cases of collision, pigeons outfitted with frosted contact lenses make it home efficiently as do normal nestmates! Thus homing can be said to rely on some function other than sight, but for the present this is all we know.

As we have seen, the artificial breeding of pigeons was originally not oriented to homing birds. Early dovecotes began to sport larger and larger inhabitants as the smaller nestlings fell to their human landlords, but with the institution of breeding for mutant color and feather specialties the real process of domestication began. An occasional pink or white mutant stood out markedly from its gray cousins and might be caught by a curious Egyptian or Greek nobleman. Bred for coloring or some other anomaly, and carefully protected from the predators that would otherwise surely have killed them off, such odd birds became favorites in the menageries of ancient times. Domestic pigeons quickly established themselves in human folklore, becoming symbols for peace, brotherhood, and other kindly affections attributed in ancient times to these murmuring herbivores. A white dove is said to have returned to the Ark with an olive branch, announcing the imminent end of that soggy journey. Even today, doves are said to be opposed to hawks on issues of internationally agonistic behavior. Interestingly, there is mounting evidence indicating that actual hawks are birds whose private lives display peace and dignity far exceeding that found among the occasionally vicious rock doves. An animal as heavily armed as a hawk must display corresponding restraint when among its own, whereas the harmless rock dove may punish its brethren relentlessly with bill and forewings over food or nesting space. This difference in behavior between herbivores and carnivores, between the habitually weaponless and the heavily armed, is general among the higher vertebrates and persists in humans. In this latter species the frequent and spectacular displays called wars are enjoyed by thousands upon thousands of humans who cheerfully labor to produce them. This enthusiastic espousal of militant causes is a result of the superimposition, on the mainly vegetarian and rather fierce primate mind, of a truly flamboyant carnivore weaponry, producing together a kind of mammalian hawk with the brains of a pigeon!

Symbols aside, humans quickly selected and maintained mutations such as changes in number of tail feathers (the normal is twelve, but some fantails achieve forty and cannot fly properly), in size, in skeletal structure (bent mandibles, giant feet, more or fewer vertebrae, longer or shorter wings), and presence or absence of facial feathers or gigantic inflatable crops. Although homing pigeons generally resemble the wild rock dove for efficiency in flight, the "fancy" breeds have reached some truly monstrous heights of inbreeding.

Pigeon fanciers group the breeds into several classes based on ancestries and collections of mutations involved. Thus one group is composed of pigeons whose ancestors showed anomalies in flight. Careful selection and maintenance of such anomalies has led to the establishment of breeds (highfliers, tumblers) whose strange aerial maneuvers are a delight to humans and to falcons, for which such twisted birds make easier prey than was ever meant to be. Highfliers, when released, collect into dense flocks at great heights—they have no choice, because this pattern has been etched into their very chromosomes—while some parlor tumblers cannot fly more than a meter above the ground without somersaulting over and over.

Despite their many physical differences, which to an uninformed observer would suggest that pigeons are actually many different species of birds, all of these domestic breeds are members of the species *Columba livia.* Throughout the species, courtship and nesting behavior are similar; and the young grow at similar rates, behave similarly upon reaching majority, prefer the same foods, and are fully fertile in breeding one race with another. Universally, rock dove courtship begins with the male's advances, billing and cooing. Billing behavior is descended from courtship feeding, a device used by birds to overcome their natural fear of bodily contact. Because of the delicacy and overawing importance of their feather covering, birds must keep clear of contact at most times, and a ritual must take place to dissipate this fear before the act of copulation. *In copulo* the male stands on, or "treads," the female, rougher handling than she will ever receive otherwise, and her trust must be gained by his feeding her beforehand. Rock doves have eliminated the actual passing of food but maintain the traditional forms in a way distinctly reminiscent of human spooning.

When a pair-bond is established, the male bird collects the few nesting materials employed by rock doves. Originally cliff dwellers, the doves prepare the nest in any suitably elevated ledge or hole, the female building a little ridge of nesting material to keep the eggs from rolling about. At copulation, the male passes some two hundred million sperm into the female, but she never lays more than three eggs at a time. In the wild, rock doves bred two times or, if lucky, three times a year; mutations selected by humans have resulted in domestic birds that breed as many as eight times a year, and these increased breeding rates are sometimes transmitted by escapees to produce similar trends in urban populations of pigeons, which increase accordingly.

Pigeon eggs hatch about eighteen days after they are laid. Even if three eggs are laid, only two squabs are raised by their parents and pigeon fanciers generally remove a third egg when it is laid. During incubation the male sits on the nest from morning until afternoon, the female at all other times. On hatching, the squab (called at this stage a squeaker, for the foolish yeeping noises it makes) is fed with the aforementioned pigeon's milk, a curdlike substance secreted from the lining of the crop of both parents and composed of approximately 72 percent water, 15 percent protein, 10 percent fat, and some 3 percent nitrogen compounds of various sorts. Pigeon's milk is rich in calcium and vitamins A, B, and B_1 and provides the squeaker's total diet for its first few days out of the egg. Production of pigeon milk is stimulated by the same hormone (prolactin) responsible for milk secretion and "motherliness" in mammals and gradually tapers off as the squeaker is fed more and more of the oily and starchy grains that make up most of the adult diet. After about ten days, production of milk ceases and the young bird subsists entirely on a diet like that of the adult. During this entire time the squab is developing feathers. Those of the head and chin are the last to appear, because the young bird must insert its head into the parent's craw to fetch his meals, but by the age of two or three weeks the squab is fully fledged and ready to leave the nest. By the end of its first five weeks, the young pigeon is independent of parental care, and the parents are ready to breed again.

Adult pigeons, living up to three decades, continue their diet of seeds, varying it only with wild fruits and an occasional scrap from human dinner tables. Because such a vegetarian diet contains almost no salt, the birds must seek this essential out. Domestic birds are provided with salt pellets containing a variety of minerals for good health, but wild rock doves must obtain their salt from such sources as human toilet areas, sewage, and the offal from around slaughterhouses. Pigeons also find essential minerals in lime and mortar, often damaging buildings and other structures by eating up the cement that holds them together.

The most obvious proof that all rock doves are one species is in the populations of North American cities, where escaped domestic birds have pooled their multifarious mutation collections to produce an inquiline very similar to the wild ancestor in form and color. In any flock of city pigeons one may distinguish the recent escapees, gaudy freaks parading unnoticed among numbers of second- and third-generation freeborn mongrel grays. The gimpy swallow-spot and stilted pouter, the flashy white and twisted tumbler, all pool genes in a frothing mixture from which emerges—hey! presto!—the original rock dove, alive and well, his very brain and behavioral structure having been stored unchanged in the collective gonads of the domesticated breeds, showing that the rock dove, *Columba livia,* is very tough and elastic genetically.

The pigeon's position as an inquiline in our largest cities remains unique in that this bird subsists on—even owes its existence to—intentional feedings by human beings. As we noted at the beginning of the chapter, the pigeon lives on love, or on some emotion on the part of city humans that approximates love. Many millions of the poorest people in the United States and around the world, people whose lives are crushed by bigotry, malnutrition, and ignorance, spend millions of dollars for the solace of a few minutes of feeding the pigeons in the park, feeling the whir of their wings, spotting individual birds with which they are acquainted from past feedings, sensing the freedom of flight above the stinking cities that lean close around them. Lonely people awaiting death from emphysema and cancer of the lungs, city diseases, lovingly feed these birds who hastened the crudding of their lungs in the first place. Children experience the immense frustration that comes with learning that you can feed them, you can get right up close to them, but you can *not* catch pigeons with your hands. Their uncanny ability to understand the precise reach of a baby, a child, an adult, and to stay *just* beyond this reach, is an adaptation gained by rock doves from long association with their loving and occasionally pigeon-eating landlords.

Whenever an extended and close symbiosis takes place between higher animals, the partners in the relationship will come to share, among other things, parasites. Because they come closest to actual human contact of any of the avian inquilines, pigeons seem to be more intimate with us on a parasite level than are house sparrows or starlings. In addition, their droppings (a pigeon may void some 2.5 kilograms—more than 5 pounds —of feces per year) accumulate about the ledges and ornamentation of buildings and statues, sometimes to a depth of several meters. It has been estimated that the average New Yorker inhales some three micrograms of dust of pigeon guano daily, which dust is a fascinating amalgam of loathsome things.

First off, and most noticeably, the stuff stinks. Couple with this the fact that, combined with water, pigeon guano will literally eat into stone, and you already have a problem. However, there are also living things in pigeon guano, things that will gladly take up residence in human beings. One of these is a fungus called *Cryptococcus neoformans,* a living fiber that causes swelling in the membranes of the human central nervous system. The death rate for persons infected with cryptococcosis is roughly thirty percent.

Another fungal inhabitant of pigeons and their feces is *Histoplasma capsulatum,* which attacks the lungs and lymphatic system and occasionally the white blood cells of humans. Its symptoms, resembling those of pneumonia, are sometimes also fatal. Aspergillosis, a disease called "pigeon feeders" by the French, is caused by growth in the lungs of pigeons and humans of a fungus called *Aspergillus fumigatus.* This fungus usually strikes individuals of low resistance, such as those experiencing a respiratory disease from some other cause. Aspergillosis is a debilitating, often chronic disease that is often passed to other birds and to mammals that eat pigeons. Moniliasis, or thrush, is another pigeon-carried fungal disease caused by the organism *Candida albicans*. It is shared by many birds and mammals including humans, especially infants, in whose mouths it produces white patches that are often quite painful.

Among viruses transmissible from pigeon to human is that causing ornithosis, an occasionally fatal disease whose symptoms resemble those of pneumonia. It is believed that ornithosis was introduced to temperate pigeon populations by imported tropical parrots—hence the disease's old name, psittacosis—but it has since taken up residence in large city pigeon populations, from whence it occasionally escapes into the surrounding human population. A form of encephalitis virus also lives among pigeons and other birds, from whom it is transmitted to humans by mosquitoes feeding on both of these vertebrate symbionts. Because viruses are elusive elements in the ecology of humanity, they tend to go unnoticed for quite some time, and there is the strong likelihood that many more viral infections of human beings are escapees from the large populations of pigeons with which we share our space. One relatively newly found viral infection is Newcastle disease, called ND by bird fanciers, which is occasionally transmitted to humans from the respiratory tracts of infected pigeons. It infects so many birds and mammals, and infection is so rapid, that ND remains second only to rabies in prevalence of virus diseases among higher vertebrates. Some infected animals carry the virus for years, even if they are dead, dressed, and frozen, and the disease is difficult to counter because of its many strains. It has no known cure.

Pigeons also share with humans a host of bacterial infections caused by streptococci, salmonellae, and other harmful bacteria. Many of these are transmitted by the feet of pigeons, or through their feces, and some may cause severe poisoning in humans. Pigeons may or may not have collected these various diseases from the humans with whom they share them, but they have certainly collected more than their share of strictly avian parasites in their travels around the world. The millions of years since the appearance of flying archosaurians have witnessed the evolution of entire communities of organisms living on and in birds.

Young wild birds inherit not only their structure and behavior but all of the parasites appropriate to their kind, and the relationship between some parasites and their birds is so close that the parasite is said to be species-specific—structurally and physiologically limited to parasitizing one species only. The parasite coevolves with and subspeciates alongside its host, and in some cases examination of the relationships between closely related parasites may assist taxonomists in tracing the paths of avian evolution. Among the Columbiformes, for instance, the extinctions of the dodo and of the American passenger pigeon, *Ectopistes migratorius,* also meant the extinctions of faunas of parasites associated with these animals only.

The ecological niches provided by the body of a rock dove are many and varied, and the living system has produced a parasite for every possibility. A single long flight feather from a rock dove may support a system of parasites composed of up to five species, each specializing in a certain area of the feather's structure. Certain lice pierce the base of the feather shaft and eat the blood within, while farther up in the hollow center of the same shaft live mites and lice feeding on the dry feather pith. Barbules at the tip of the vane are delicately mown out by squadrons of chewing lice, even as microscopic mites consume the tiny hooks *between* the barbules, causing "feather rot" and impairing flight in some cases. Between feathers, other mites clean up the debris from the erosion of epidermis and feathers, while yet others of different species patrol the feathers of the head only, or the throat, or the warm places beneath the wings.

Fleas and lice dodge artfully among the bases of feathers, sharing with strategically attached ticks the blood and labor of the pigeon and, ultimately, the gross national product of whatever human group supports the bird in the first place. Pigeon flies, living in the nests of rock doves, bite both birds and humans, producing welts all out of proportion to their small size. Also mining the avian surface for blood are various mites, including one, the vicious chigger, that is as happy to dine on humans as on rock doves. Some mites go so far as to pierce the skin of the bird and burrow into the body cavity, while others live only in the nostrils or among the scales of the feet. Within the respiratory system of the rock dove are air sac mites, minuscule beasts that crawl about the linings of the lungs and airsacs, causing the bird to weaken and gasp. The eggs of these horrible animals are coughed up by their hosts and distributed on the dust of the air.

The life cycles of most rock dove parasites must be intimately timed to that of the host bird. Changes in the blood content of rock doves at breeding time trigger a breeding response in blood-feeding lice and mites, which time their own breeding so that young parasites may hatch and move on to young pigeons at precisely the proper moment. Blood changes preceding molting are monitored by many feather parasites, which must avoid being separated from their hosts by the shedding of feathers. Most rock dove parasites are so dependent upon the host that a short separation will kill the parasites.

But it is among the many internal parasites of rock doves that the closest parasite-pigeon symbioses take place. For example, the seed-eating habits of pigeons permit the spread of worms that spend part of their life cycles in isopods (sow bugs or pill bugs, actually land-dwelling crustaceans). Because the pigeon is a vegetarian, it would not normally encounter such worms, but isopods of many species curl up into hard little balls when disturbed. These may be eaten by pigeons mistaking them for seeds, and it is through specifically these isopods that stomach-wall worms of pigeons are most commonly distributed to the rock dove population. Insects whose main defense is curling into balls are also vectors of pigeon parasites such as eyeworms, which live in these insects for part of their life cycles. When a pigeon eats such an insect, the worm travels up the bird's esophagus and into the eye through the tear glands. Parasitic flatworms called flukes inhabit snails, on which pigeons occasionally mistakenly dine. These worms are hermaphrodites, laying thousands of eggs that pass out with the pigeon's feces. If the eggs are fortunate enough to land near water, they hatch into a swimming larval form called a miracidium, which locates a snail through a supremely sensitive snail-locating olfactory apparatus. The miracidium encysts itself within the snail, living on the snail's body fluids until it changes into a cercaria, another swimming form, which locates a second snail, where it matures into a metacercaria. If this snail is eaten by a pigeon, the fluke's life cycle is completed by reproduction in the bird's intestines, which may be inhabited by hundreds of flukes.

Some internal pigeon parasites may be transmitted by other, external, parasites from pigeon to pigeon. The common pigeon tapeworm appears to be transmitted in this way; as pigeons pick the irritating lice from their skin, they may accidentally ingest one who carries some tapeworm larvae, which mature and reproduce in the pigeon intestine. Such tapeworms may reach a meter in length within the pigeon, most of this length being composed of reproductive packets called proglottids, which are dropped with the pigeon's feces to reinfest lice and start the cycle anew. Mosquitoes and other biting arthropods similarly serve as vectors for pigeon parasites, passing skin filaria worms, malaria, pigeon pox, various forms of encephalitis, and probably many more diseases among birds and occasionally between birds and humans. Ticks, hippoboscid and black flies, and mites share in the tasks of transmitting endoparasites from one bird to another—in any single pigeon fly may reside the larvae of dozens of nematode worms parasitic on pigeons. All in all, the rock dove supports hundreds of species of smaller animals, whose stowaway existence seems to have

A falcon, the main predator of wild rock doves. The raptor shares the broad shoulders, pointed wings, and powerful flight of its prey.

gone unsuspected by the keepers of dovecotes for thousands of years until the invention of the microscope and modern parasitology.

What originally seems to have attracted humans to rock doves was the doves' graceful and elegant flight. Rock doves evolved in habitats where their strongest predators were falcons, birds specialized in the art of snatching fast-flying prey out of the air, and the coevolution of pigeons and falcons has resulted in a sort of convergence between the two. As each produced a new strategy in flight, the other has been forced to offset that strategy with a new one of its own in order to survive. This resonance between the orders Columbiformes and Falconiformes has produced two of the finest fliers in the world, both displaying a quick, short-stroked rowing flight with pointed wings that enables them to cover unbelievable distances in moments. Such masterful flight could not help but have attracted the admiration and respect of generations of humans, and both pigeons and falcons have carved fair niches for themselves in the world of human folklore. However, it is only recently that careful analyses of the mechanics

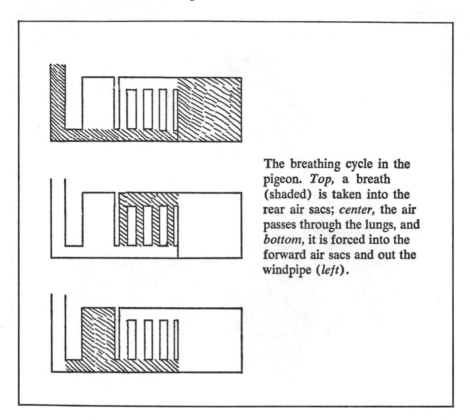

The breathing cycle in the pigeon. *Top,* a breath (shaded) is taken into the rear air sacs; *center,* the air passes through the lungs, and *bottom,* it is forced into the forward air sacs and out the windpipe (*left*).

and physiology of rock dove flight have revealed some of its secrets. We now know that the pigeon represents, along with other flying birds, the apex of evolution in terms of respiratory and circulatory systems, those directly responsible for the maintenance of the characteristically high avian rate of metabolism.

The activity called flying, in which an animal is pitted against gravity with no intervening earth against which to brace itself, is probably the most demanding activity possible for vertebrates. Birds have coped with the increased oxygen demand by evolving a respiratory system in which a continuous flow of fresh oxygen-rich air is passed through, rather than in-and-out of, the lungs. Whereas in nonflying quadrupeds (and bats) the lung itself expands and contracts to move air, in birds the lung is relatively rigid and the air pump is provided by a system of air sacs extending through most of the body cavity and even into the long bones of the wings and legs. A flying pigeon is actually a set of open-ended bubbles, a froth of organic matter through which air is perpetually moving. Air taken through the nostrils and mouth is first passed down the trachea, through the syrinx, and into the posterior air sacs (see diagram), which expand to produce this flow. Next, these posterior air sacs contract, forcing the air through the pigeon's lungs, which are composed of a spongy matrix of microscopic air capillaries in which is embedded a system of nearly parallel open-ended tubules called parabronchi. Moving through the parabronchi, the air passes oxygen to the blood vessels permeating the air capillaries, picking up carbon dioxide in return from the blood. Passing on through the lungs, the air is sucked into the forward air sacs by their expansion, and finally expelled through the trachea and mouth by the contraction of these sacs. In the meantime, another gust of air has moved through the lungs, and in this manner the air capillaries are always awash with fresh air; there is no period of stagnancy between inhalation and exhalation, and the flying bird is assured oxygen commensurate with its need.

In addition to performing as superchargers for the respiratory system, the rock dove's air sacs function as a cooling system to convey most of the immense amount of heat generated in flight to the outside of the bird. A flying city pigeon may produce thirty times as much heat as it does resting, and less than a quarter of the air inhaled goes to respiration. The rest of this air is diverted through air sacs alongside all of the major organs in the body cavity and across the inner sides of the powerful muscles of flight, conducting heat away and out of the bird. The smooth flow through these air sacs assures a rapid heat transmission at their moist inner surfaces, which in a pigeon may total more than a square meter, so that the bird is cooled by a form of internal sweating. If the brain of a pigeon is raised in temperature, the breathing rate increases correspondingly to cause greater evaporative cooling at the air-sac surfaces. In response to temperature changes the breath rate of a pigeon may vary from as low as forty to more than five hundred per minute.

In such a high-powered animal as the rock dove, moving oxygen from the point of capture at the lungs to the point of use at each of the billions of living cells in the organism requires a circulatory system able to move large volumes of blood at high pressures and velocities. At the heart of this seething system is, of course, the bird's heart. The archosaurian heart, like that of mammals, represents a significant departure from that of the rest of the vertebrates in that it actually consists of two double-chambered pumps laid side by side at the center of the circulatory system.

In the rock dove the left ventricle of the heart must drive the blood at high pressure through the entire circulatory system excepting only the lungs, beating as much as two hundred times per minute in so doing (compared with the human rate of about seventy-two times per minute). The muscular walls of this half of the pump are some three times as massive as those of the right, which circulates blood only through the lungs. The pressure generated by the left ventricle may be as much as ten times that of the right, especially during times of stress. Rock doves approach the limits of mechanical safety for blood pressure with this surging pump, such that a suddenly frightened pigeon may die of a ruptured heart or aorta.

We have observed that the force providing our inquiline rock doves with the means of survival in urban situations is a human force, one of affection. This affection seems due, at least in part, to the spectacular falcon-designed flight of these birds, a locomotion which has touched the hearts of humanity for thousands of years. Most of us have flown in our dreams, sighing through the silent air among the skyscrapers, dropping delicately into the streets and yards of our cities. A few of us manage to soar in the great silent sailplanes of the rich, seeking the thermals on which hawks and eagles ride, hoping in this way to partake of the feeling of true flight. A great many humans are catapulted through the sky in streamlined capsules at 1000 kilometers per hour, 10 or 12 kilometers above the earth, each day—but such flight is more akin to the passage of a bullet, and the sensations of air passengers are more like those of the passengers in a railroad train than they are like those that must be experienced by a pigeon kneading the air in a bright city morning. So, in our envy, we continue to support the unproductive multitude of doves, contracting their diseases and wondering how the hell they are able to move about in the air with such unspeakable grace and ease when we, the lords of creation, remain bound by gravity and machinery to our earthly concerns.

The act of avian flight is far too complex for present human understanding to comprehend, but an analysis of its fundamentals may greatly increase our pleasure in feeding city pigeons. Actually, while operating under a few broad aerodynamic principles, the flying bird is so intricately molded to its medium that it can be said to be a bit of denser air moving through the atmosphere around it. Still, we can see some of the fundamentals of flight plainly enough while sitting on a park bench, and readers might lug this book and some bread out to the nearest place occupied by a number of free *Columba livia* (it can't be far) to take a lesson in flight from the birds.

Flight on earth began with the insects, perhaps three hundred million years ago. Insect flight is vastly different from that of birds—after all, insects are arthropods, whose skeletons are on the outside and whose breath must diffuse slowly through their body tissues without the aid of any sophisticated metabolic systems of the sort we have just examined in pigeons. Still, many insects are elegant fliers within the limits imposed by their sluggish arthropod metabolisms, and it was the ability to fly that gave them effective dominion of the living system—a dominion compared to which our own vaunted superiority is but a momentary anomaly.

Since they were the first fliers, insects early exploited nearly every ecological niche imaginable and continue to do so to this day. Insect wings evolved from thoracic flaps that enabled early hexapods (six-leggers) to glide away from their predators. In no way are insect wings homologous to the wings of birds, for they evolved quite independently of any other struc-ture and are unique to class Insecta.

For about two hundred million years insects were the only flying animals on the planet. Being the sole occupants of the atmospheric sea, they quickly diverged in form and function, often reaching the size of modern hawks as they moved into newer and more advanced roles of predation and escape. During the heyday of the amphibians among the vertebrates, long before the advent of even reptiles, dragonflies with meter-wide wingspreads captured similarly impressive stoneflies over the carbonif-erous swamps, occasionally falling in the process, to be captured in the mud and to have their forms read hundreds of millions of years later by the humans who mine the coal that is all that remains of the primordial swamps.

A hundred or so million years after their appearance on the evolu-tionary scene, flying insects had radiated so successfully into the air that a considerable biomass was occupied in flying about in the incarnation of insects. These insects represented a vast protein resource to any larger form innovative enough to take to the air after them. In retrospect it seems in-evitable that the vertebrates should have exploited this opportunity, but at the time, the first vertebrate aeronauts represened a giant step in quadruped evolution. Earliest of these flying vertebrates were those animals that first developed an elongated fourth finger supporting a gliding surface of skin. Unlike birds, these animals may have descended from primitive archosaur-ians that still walked on four feet rather than two, so that the wing retained a walking function and was equipped with three strongly differentiated claws for climbing about. This early vertebrate pterodactyl (wing-finger) arrangement created a simple cambered-plane wing surface, with which its possessors soared lightly on the breeze. Strong and efficient flight

A pterosaur catches the wind on pointed wings. Such animals were inefficient at best in situations where erratic winds and obstacles required finer control.

muscles permitted the occasional flapping needed to best exploit air currents, but the wing-finger crowd enjoyed a rather passive form of flight in general.

In these animated kites, which are called pterosaurs, "winged lizards," by paleontologists even though they were not lizards, the wing was long and narrow and supported by only one strut with which the structure cut the air. This sort of wing provided the airfoil shape which creates lift by passing air over an upper surface that is longer than the lower surface, lowering the air pressure on the upper surface so that the pressure on the lower surface pushes the whole arrangement up. It is a relatively primitive and inflexible system, most familiarly demonstrated by the wings of airplanes. It is probable that pterosaurs spent most of their time in open areas where the wind blew fairly constantly. Most pterosaur fossils are found in seashore contexts, and it seems that they soared albatrosslike, living sails up to 10 meters across, over the vast oceans of the Mesozoic. In such environments they were always able to locate the winds with which most of their flight was powered, and thus to maintain the high airspeed necessary to maintain control with such narrow wings. Early pterosaurs exploited the matter and energy locked into the larger flying insects, perhaps fortunately driving these huge arthropods into extinction, and then moved on to fish. For many millions of years vertebrate flight seems to have been limited to environments where most of the wind was high and the flying open.

Exploitation of the rest of the world's airspace by vertebrates had to await the development of a more sophisticated wing, one which would provide not only lift but also propulsion over long periods of time. Pterosaurs needed good winds and a lot of space to function really efficiently; over land the winds tend to be erratic and localized in effect, and obstructions such as trees and rocks abound. Also, if you want to land on the mainland you have to be able to take off again quickly, for predators are rife there. Pterosaurs were weak walkers at best and show every sign of having *never* landed except on isolated cliffs and islands, again in the manner of albatrosses today.

The little bipeds that first evolved quilled feathers solved with this nuance all of the problems of the pterosaur wing. Animals like Archaeopteryx, discussed in the chapter on house sparrows, seem to have been terrestrial creatures; they could not really fly, or even soar very far, and if downed over water would have little chance to lift off again. On land, however, they were elegantly quick runners in the manner of most archosaurian bipeds, and their gliding feather surfaces seem to have evolved to permit their predatory way of life to continue as the larger, slower insects were depleted by their successes. In addition, they had to contend with larger archosaurian predators, from which their new airfoils allowed them a better chance to escape. In an aerial situation one must have the tightest control imaginable, simply to avoid slamming into tree limbs, let alone catching weensy little insects on the glide. In the still forest air of their origins, the early feathered wings offered far more command than could the narrow wings of pterosaurs.

In order to maintain lift in a slowing airspeed, a long pointed wing such as that of a pterosaur must increase its angle of incidence to the moving air, thus increasing pressure beneath the wing sharply. In so doing, however, the wing creates turbulence on its upper surface as the air flows and eddies over the leading edge, finally bringing the entire structure to a halt as the angle of incidence reaches the stalling angle. Now, if a small airfoil is placed above and in front of the wing, creating a slot through which air is constricted and thus speeded smoothly over the wing's upper surface, the turbulence is sharply decreased and the wing continues lifting at its top surface. To facilitate landing accurately on branches or ledges, early feathered archosaurian gliders acquired an alula, a feather winglet mounted on the thumb and providing the very slot necessary for such accuracy. With the acquisition of the alula true avian flight, the finest in the world, was born and the function of the avian forelimb became only that of flight. The necessity to protect the alula caused the manipulative functions of the arm to be shelved and the arm itself, now a true wing, to be folded safely and compactly away when not in use. The evolution of slotting was further refined with the ability of birds to separate and turn the feathers of the wingtip, the primaries, so that each provided slotting for the next, to permit extremely precise, slow glides.

We noted that on land the wind is unpredictable at best, and in such a situation birds were helpless until they developed true powered flight of the sort best exemplified by the rock dove. Watching pigeons in the park you will notice that they actually glide only rarely; when they do, it is a fairly rapid downward slide over the air on sharply dihedral (angled) wings. Most pigeon flight is the rapid rowing movement in which the wing-tips actually travel a figure eight in relation to the bird's body. On the downstroke, powered by the heavy major pectorals, the pigeon wing actually moves forward while the primary feathers of the "hand" strike sharply downward. Air is squeezed from beneath the trailing wing surface by the descending primaries, creating a strong forward thrust. At the bottom of their motion the primaries spread apart and twist, each providing forward thrust in the manner of the blade of an airplane propeller. By this time the forearm has already begun the upstroke, and the primaries slot further apart to reduce air resistance on the way up, the whole primary/hand assembly snapping after the forearm in the quickest movement of the cycle. At this point the primaries are slotted like a wide-open Venetian blind, allowing most air to pass through them, and as the wing moves backward and upward to its peak the primaries follow and rotate together again into a solid plane that begins the next stroke downward. During the entire cycle the primaries have provided most of the propulsive effect, while the secondaries along the forearm provide lift with their airfoil surface so that the pigeon really gets around.

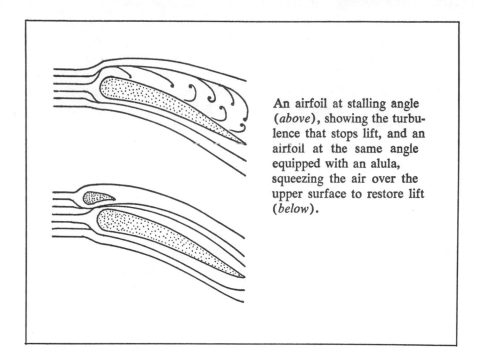

An airfoil at stalling angle (*above*), showing the turbulence that stops lift, and an airfoil at the same angle equipped with an alula, squeezing the air over the upper surface to restore lift (*below*).

Against such competition the pterosaurs could not stand, and seabirds replaced them as the success of birds on land produced selective pressure forcing some birds to seashores and beyond. In response to the demands of the ocean environment modern seabirds in many cases parallel the form of the pterosaurs, as in the case of the albatross, even to the point of having secondarily lost both the ability to slot their wing feathers and the ability to walk worth a damn. It is nice to think that in the seabirds of today we may dimly recall the endless Mesozoic oceans and the majestic sailing of Pteranodon and its wing-fingered kin before the triumph of the feather.

Back on land, however, where flying is flying, the art of powered flight has reached its zenith in the competitive coevolution of predators and their prey. Both pigeons and falcons, which traditionally fed on pigeons (but which, under the influence of humanity, will soon be extinct), share the fastest and the bestest of equipage for hurtling through the air. In addition to wings whose operation is so complex that we have barely begun to unravel their secrets even with high-speed strobe photography, these birds share a teardrop-shaped body form, which permits the most efficient high-speed parting of the fluid air. The teardrop shape can be altered, however, to suit conditions, and a pigeon applying his brakes can be seen to flatten his breast and widen his contours to present a nearly plane surface perpendicular to his direction of movement. His tail, serving as a rudder in full flight, becomes a spread fan, an airbrake to add to his surface, and wham! he is afoot, a little dinosaur walking about as his terrestrial ancestors did a hundred million years ago, ambling up to partake of the bread you offer him.

It is small wonder that the rock dove, with its spectacular powers of flight, ability to return home over vast distances and colorful history, has achieved its unique ecological status as the only protected inquiline of the artificial system. Modern understanding of the bird's role in urban pollution and diseases has not deterred the millions of pigeon-feeders, who continue to contribute to the increase of urban *C. livia* around the world. Attempts to control city pigeon populations seem doomed to failure, for pigeon-feeders wax militant when their beloved birds are threatened by the activity of sanitation officials. The protection offered these pigeons by their human admirers, plus the never-ending trickle of escapees from domestic stock, probably assures these birds a safe place among us for as long as our cities remain habitable by vertebrates—a time span fairly open to question.

4 The Mouse

U pon a time far away, twelve thousand summers perhaps, certain small and tidy rodents lived among grasses whose seeds they ate, in the prairies of a new land. These were relatively new rodents, evolved for a time when the ice of past millennia was receding before a new warmth, shortening the winter and melting the permafrost of a portion of Eurasia. The grasses flourished in the summer sun and the little rodents that lived among the grasses flourished also, and with them hawks and owls and mammals and snakes, and special fleas and flies, all perfectly designed to feed on the plant-caught sun distilled so magnificently into Rodent.

And into this land there came nomadic humans, hunters and often fisherfolk, eaters of grass seed when they could gather enough to mash into a paste and bake near the fire. Eventually, the humans abandoned their nomadic ways, cleared and then cultivated the land. Hawks and owls and rodent-eating mammals and snakes went elsewhere, but the rodents, tiny seed-eaters, stayed on. And in the time-honored manner of all life, the humans and rodents reproduced enough to offset predation—but there were ever fewer predators. Many more human young lived to eat more and more of the plants grown by their elders, and many more little rodents lived in the homes and storage rooms of the humans, expanding into a rodent wonderland of food-filled predator-free space. Thus with the birth of agriculture was born the house mouse, paradigm of mousedom, named *Mus musculus,* "Mouse littlemouse," by Linnaeus.

House mice are members of the largest and one of the newest families of the mammalian class, the Muridae, "mouselike ones," to which they give their name. Murids are a brilliantly successful family of rodents ranging from mouse-sized mice to rabbit-sized rats, and believed to have first separated from ancestral rodent stock during the Miocene period ten to fifteen million years ago. Omnivorous diet and awesome powers of reproduction enabled murids to spread quickly across the Eurasian and African continents, and even into Australia, where murids are the only native placental mammals besides bats. Depending on which taxonomist you prefer, the Muridae comprise ninety to a hundred genera, some three hundred and eighty species, and perhaps fifteen hundred subspecies of spectacularly prosperous little mammals, including not only house mice but the famous murid rats of the next chapter.

Murids have refined the characteristics that have made rodents the most numerous and successful of mammals. The order Rodentia, the "gnawers," to which murids belong, contains more than half of all described mammalian species. Rodents eat more, reproduce faster, and have shorter life spans than the members of any other mammalian order. Because of a fairly primitive and generalized body plan and extremely short generations, the rodents show incredible genetic flexibility and seemingly infinite variation in form and function.

Individual species of rodents range in size from that of the pygmy mouse, which weighs about 4 grams (0.14 ounce), to that of the South American capybara, which weighs in at 50 kilograms (more than 100 pounds) and measures more than a meter in length. Within this range there are more than three thousand species of rodents, representing three hundred or more genera. Rodents early left the basic mammalian insectivore stock to become the great, distinctive order of modern times. In many respects they have retained characteristics of the earliest true mammals, and *Mus musculus* exhibits many of these in both form and function. Like many other rodents, murids retain a remnant of the old reptilian scaly coat in their bare, scaled tails. House mice possess a body skeleton that differs little from that of the earliest mammals, and the articulation of the bones of the hands and feet remains nearly identical to that of the first mammals of the Mesozoic era. By taking a careful look at a normal house mouse we may reconstruct some of the long history of the mammalian class, which has produced not only mice but men.

The ancestors of mammals diverged from reptilian stock at the very

Restoration of *Dimetrodon*, with the solar heating equipment that was one of the earliest experiments in temperature control by the ancestors of the mammals.

beginning of reptilian evolution, as far back as two hundred and eighty million years ago. The earliest mammallike reptiles, or synapsids, appeared in a time when the first vertebrates freed their reproductive cycles from dependence on bodies of water by inventing the reptilian egg. With this momentous event, vertebrates in the reptile pattern exploded across the lands of the earth, slipping rapidly into ever newer and more specialized niches as their options increased. During this unprecedented radiation of vertebrate species, many new metabolic forms were undergoing experimentation as selective pressure for some sort of internal temperature control became more intense.

The earliest synapsids were pelycosaurs, reptiles whose teeth were already beginning to show the differentiation characteristic of their mammalian descendants. These animals also show some signs of early experimentation with sophisticated temperature-control systems, notably in the famous *Dimetrodon*, whose "sail" is believed to have been a temperature-control device. When the broad surface of the sail was oriented perpendicular to the rays of the sun, *Dimetrodon* could quickly absorb enough early morning heat to be up and about ahead of most other larger animals. This was an advantage in that *Dimetrodon* was a carnivore and could easily steal up on its sluggishly cold relatives during the early daylight hours. Also reflective of a higher level of activity than is possible in other reptiles is the evolution in pelycosaurs of limbs and limb girdles that permitted a more efficient mode of locomotion. In *Dimetrodon* the legs are partly swung beneath the body rather than sprawled sideways as in more primitive reptiles, and it is apparent that, though ungainly looking at best, Dimetrodon could move fast and effectively once warmed with its solar sail.

Around two hundred and fifty million years ago the first therapsids, our earliest-known truly warm-blooded ancestors, appear in the fossil record. Although there was for a time a dispute among paleontologists as to the sort of metabolism possessed by these immensely successful animals, the question has been resolved with studies similar to those on dinosaur metabolism discussed in the chapter on house sparrows. Therapsids radiated into many specialized forms but shared a generally mammalian structure, with relatively strong, efficient legs firmly set under a lithe and active trunk. While the brain remained relatively small and the lower jaw primitive in structure, therapsids continued the dental evolution begun by the pelycosaurs. In exploiting the many niches opening to endothermic animals, the therapsids gradually acquired tooth specializations approaching the diversity of those of their descendants, the modern mammals, and we can assume that when they eventually became dominant they were among the most advanced of terrestrial animals.

Unfortunately for the march of mammalian evolution, another class made it to true warm-bloodedness and thus to dominance of the vertebrate ecology just a little bit earlier than the therapsids. The archosaurians appeared during the Permian period, about two hundred and forty million years ago, making their entrance in the form of smallish bipeds or partly bipedal forms called thecodonts. The evolution of warm-bloodedness on their part came entirely independently of that in the therapsids, and perhaps more rapidly; at any rate, by the end of the Triassic, in the middle of the Mesozoic period, roughly one hundred and ninety million years ago, the process was complete. The four-footed, scent-oriented therapsids, with an as-yet imperfectly developed system of walking, were superseded by the bipedal archosaurians, whose front feet were efficient grasping organs. And so during the Mesozoic era, mammals were relegated to a timid, mouselike existence with a life spent in and around dark places where the fast, sharp-eyed archosaurians rarely went.

Still, it seems that it was during their period of relative insignificance, through the rolling ages of the Mesozoic, that mammals underwent their greatest changes from the old reptilian pattern. It is likely that the therapsids still laid eggs like reptiles. A couple of marginal mammalian species of Australia, the platypus and echidna, continue to lay eggs today, but it was probably fairly early in the Mesozoic that small marsupials—metatherians—and placental mammals—eutherians—made their independent appearances on the evolutionary scene. Eggs are highly vulnerable creatures requiring either careful concealing or parental protection from egg-eaters. These beasts shared the innovation of having eliminated from their reproductive cycle the egg as an independent entity. In both metatherians and eutherians the egg is retained within the mother's body until the youngster hatches, and consequently the shell became superfluous and eventually disappeared. Further, in some metatherians and all eutherians the developing young is directly connected to the maternal metabolic system by means of a placenta, an organ derived from one of the membranes of the old egg, which transmits nutrients and oxygen from the mother's body to that of the infant and passes wastes from infant to mother. In this fashion it became unnecessary for mammals to hang around and protect a bunch of fragile eggs.

Even with this advantage over archosaurians, the early mammals remained in the background. Throughout the Mesozoic neither metatherians nor eutherians experienced much radiation in body form, but the teeth of both groups acquired enough specialization to spread them around the world. One early Jurassic form, *Taeniolabis,* was a herbivore with a gnawing dentition strongly suggestive of the rodents yet to come, and others approximated small modern carnivores in dentition and build. The form of one such marsupial of the Cretaceous period eighty million years ago has survived unchanged in the living American opossum *Didelphis,* a tree-dweller that offers us a good look at what mammalian conditions were like in those distant times. Like the opossum, mammals of the Mesozoic were rarely bigger than a modern house cat, small of brain and long of snout, with relatively small eyes and advanced olfactory centers. They were largely nocturnal and inconspicuous and relied on their noses to accomplish most of what they had to do, a natural outcome of their preference for trees and roots and the dark hours.

Early mammals seem to have been flatfooted (plantigrade) climbers with five long digits on all four feet. For ease in climbing one digit—the first—tended toward opposability so that the little climbers might grab safely in the night and cling to the narrowest of twigs. For millions of years both metatherians and eutherians continued in this inconspicuous fashion, but with the gradual decline in the number of archosaurian species toward the end of the Cretaceous, both groups began to undergo the radiation that would ultimately bring them dominance.

The metatherians, which carried their young in marsupia (pouches), were early bested in competition for ecological niches by the eutherians, whose more efficient placentas and more highly organized nervous systems permitted them to drive metatherians to the peripheral continents of Australia and South America. These continents became separated from the rest of the earth's landmasses sometime during the late Cretaceous period, so that their metatherian populations continued to thrive and diversify while becoming extinct in Eurasia, Africa, and North America. South America has rejoined and separated from North America several times since, developing in the meantime a strange mixture of primitive and modern eutherians, but its metatherian population has dwindled to a meager few dull opossums in the process. The American opossum already mentioned is a recent immigrant from South America, and has recently greatly enlarged its range as a result of the activities of European humans in North America. As will be discussed in a later chapter, the opossum is well on its way to becoming an inquiline in artificial ecological situations, but it is a faint echo of the rich metatherian population of South America during the early part of the mammalian ascendancy.

In Australia, isolated as it was from the eutherian competition of the rest of the world, metatherians radiated into every niche available to mammals, evolving ecological counterparts to much of the eutherian evolution of the other continents. When European humans first arrived on that island continent they found marsupial "wolves," "squirrels," "bears," "mice," and others, all strikingly resembling their mainland placental counterparts. While grazing placentals in other parts of the world evolved the ruminant stomach capable of digesting cellulose by means of mutualism with microorganisms in the rumen of the stomach, grazing marsupials in Australia paralleled this development with another such mutualism, another fancy stomach/microorganism system. To escape predation, grazing placentals evolved high-speed running on all fours, with specially modified legs, while in Australia the grazers developed a bipedal leap on highly modified hind legs. These marsupials became, of course, the kangaroos of today, remarkable parallels to the antelopes and bovines on the placental mainland.

Australia's isolation continued to modern times, over seventy million years of evolution. During this time the only placentals to have reached that continent unaided by humans—a continent that for terrestrial animals might as well have been another planet—were the fliers (bats) and a few gnawers (murid rodents) that may have clung to floating logs.

Among placentals, the Cretaceous stock of insectivores provided the trunk of the evolutionary tree. Insectivores continue nearly unchanged from the late Cretaceous to modern times in the form of shrews and moles and other animals sharing the climbing and burrowing habits of the earliest mammals. Closely related to the insectivores and sharing their same general plan are the bats, order Chiroptera, which took to the air early in the evolution of mammals. Also similar to the insectivores in their primitive, unspecialized body plan are the primates, descendants of climbing insectivores something like the tree shrew. Even the bipedal humans, with their giant brains and small teeth, retain the old insectivore form nearly bone for bone, modified though it is by millions of years spent in trees by our primate ancestors.

Rodents also left the insectivore stock early, so early, in fact, that the earliest rodent fossil known, that of *Paramys,* "sort-of-a-mouse," of the Paleocene, sixty-five million years ago, represents a true rodent in the modern sense with no transitional insectivore characteristics. *Paramys* appears to have been a ratlike burrower similar in size and general construction to the murid *Rattus norvegicus* of modern times. While the insectivore body plan is retained in rodents in general, it is the head that distinguishes the order from all other mammals, and that is responsible for their ultimate success. The rodent skull is designed around gnawing equipment consisting of the four incisor (cutting) teeth, two on the upper jaw and two on the lower. These teeth are designed such that they grow constantly, up to 5 centimeters a year in the house mouse, as long as their possessor is alive. To counter this incessant growth, the teeth are so arranged that their front side is covered with hard enamel and their posterior half composed of softer dentin, which wears in use. Thus these remarkable incisors, which always wear uppers against lowers, are forever sharp and can penetrate nearly any substance evolved by vegetation to stop them. Behind the incisors is a diastema, or gap, where the other incisors and the canines of the insectivores were located before they were lost forever by the ancestors of the rodents. To the rear of the diastema is a variable set of grinding teeth to masticate the material rent apart by the incisors.

Operating the gnawing teeth is an arrangement of jaw muscles that has set the form of the rodent skull off even more sharply from that of other mammals. The masseter muscle, which descends from the cheekbone to the jaw in humans and most other mammals, is in the rodent divided into three parts designed to give the lower jaw movement from side to side, forward and back, and round and round, as well as in the usual hinged jawbone swing. Successive waves of rodents have altered the arrangement of the parts of the masseter to such a degree that we have been able to classify the order into (about) three large suborders based on the arrangement of this one muscle.

Most primitive of these rodent suborders is the Sciuromorpha, "squirrel-shaped ones," of whom the true squirrels are but a specialized offshot. The sewellel or "mountain beaver" of California and the northwestern United States is the most primitive rodent alive, a sciuromorph little changed from the days of *Paramys*. Ground squirrels, arboreal squirrels, and a few others are classed in this suborder, whose teeth and jaw muscles have changed little since the rodents first appeared.

Descendants of sciuromorphs isolated during one of South America's disconnections from the rest of the world evolved yet another way of stringing the floating rodent jawbone to produce efficient chewing. These became the Caviomorpha, "guinea-pig-like ones," a strictly South American group whose only members to reach North America are the American porcupine and, of course, the domesticated cavy or guinea pig. During millions of years of isolation in South America these animals radiated into some strange places, producing the giant capybara, a sort of aquatic pig-rat (see illustration), and small cavies rather resembling miniature deer. Although a marginal group, evolutionarily speaking, the caviomorphs did produce the guinea pig, which was domesticated by the Andean Amerindians and which no longer survives in the wild.

There are some rodents that defy classification into either of these suborders and miss the third by a long shot, so we may squeeze them in here. The beavers, an ancient group originally specialized toward bur-

The capybara, largest of rodents, weighs in at some 50 kilograms (110 pounds).

rowing and often combining this way of life with a marked fondness for water, in ancient times sometimes approached the size of modern bears. Modern beavers are all aquatic and often profoundly alter the landscape by felling trees and damming streams. Next to humans they are probably the most skilled of animals in creating large environments to suit their own tastes, although the design of their earthworks and waterworks appears to be inborn and largely automatic. In addition to beavers there are rodents in Africa that seem to stand alone in the order's taxonomy. Certain cane and rock "rats" and the Old World porcupine seem to have no close affinities among living rodents and are usually left unclassified or placed into a suborder of their own, the Hystricomorpha, "porcupinelike ones."

The third great currently recognized rodent suborder, the Myomorpha, exceed all the rest combined in number of genera and species. Named "mouse-shaped ones" for their best-known representatives, the myomorphs appear to have originated later than the other suborders, but by the Pliocene epoch between ten million and one million years ago they had become the most abundant of rodents. Among modern myomorphs are the jerboas and jumping mice of the Old World, desert-adapted animals that hop on their hind legs, and Eurasian dormice, American gophers and kangaroo rats, and certain burrowing rats of the Eastern Hemisphere that, because of their habits, are similar to moles in form. But the group of myomorphs primarily responsible for the suborder's great success is the superfamily Muroidae, "those-who-are-like-mice," the "true" rats and mice that inhabit every continent and nearly every island of the globe. These represent the root stock and most successful offshoots of the myomorphs. The earliest muroids descended from sciuromorphs in the early Oligocene about forty million years ago and radiated from their place of origin in the Eastern Hemisphere in the form of two great families, the Cricetidae, "hamsterlike ones," and the Muridae, the largest family of mammals, the Old World rats and mice.

The cricetids represent all native North American rats and mice, including deer mice, grasshopper mice, wood rats, harvest mice, voles, and others familiar to inhabitants of rural North America. In addition, Syrian hamsters, gerbils, and other Old World rodents are cricetids, and some of these have been semidomesticated and rather spread about in recent years by human activity.

The murids evolved in the tropics of Eurasia and northern Africa, where they adapted to an existence dependent on seeds and fruits. Unlike most rodents, murids also show a tendency toward either omnivory or active carnivory at times, and the resultant catholicity of their tastes has been in large part responsible for their immense success. Murids possess four fingers and a thumb knob on the forefoot, which is designed for grasping as well as walking. The hindfoot is five-toed, little removed in structure from that of the earliest fossil mammals except for webbing between the toes in certain cases. There are seven subfamilies of murids, all but one of which are still confined to the Eastern Hemisphere. Members of three or four species of that one subfamily, the Murinae, left the confines of their ancestral home only with the coming of agriculture and ships. In the company of humanity these few species of this one family have become the most numerous and widespread mammals on the planet, precisely duplicating the range of humanity with such efficiency that they now constitute the entire wild land mammal fauna of Antarctica. They share with us the pinnacle of success and will no doubt continue on that pinnacle for some time after our demise. They are supremely competent at the game of life, economical, adaptable, genetically changeable, and generally good at the business of living, and of all animals other than humans they are the most feared and hated by humans.

In general, murids preserve the primitive mammalian form. This generalized physique, with proper adjustments for size, allows them to exploit any environment in which there is enough warmth and harborage (hiding space) in which to rear their young. Those murids that reproduce the fastest are of the smallest size, best able to survive under conditions where populations may be dense. In such conditions family groups are formed and remain intact over many generations, and systems of social defense may evolve in response to environmental pressures. Some murids have evolved fairly complex social structures that enable them to exploit new habitats more easily, and it was from these social forms that our inquiline rats and mice evolved.

The original *Mus musculus* was a burrower, living in places where vegetable cover and food were always available. Mice tended to enlarge the burrows of their parents, such that entire warrens of tunnels inhabited by large family groups resulted. All of the mice in such groups retain a recognizable scent, and communities of mice are able to recognize co-citizens by scent alone. Although each mouse in a community may build its own nest, these individual nests are not defended from fellow community citizens. On the other hand, communities defend their burrowed territory against outgroup mice (those from other communities) with vigor, and the boundaries of territories are carefully and repeatedly delineated by scent marks at urination points along the periphery. This hostility toward out-group mice ensures a certain amount of genetic isolation between families and permits the rapid subspeciation and adaptation to varying environments characteristic of the species.

Within mouse communities there is an order of dominance recognized among the males of the group. Although this pecking order is carefully observed by the group members, it can be (and often is) disputed and an alpha or dominant male routed by one of his subordinates. Female mice are not part of the hierarchy but are subordinate to most males because of the males' greater size and mass. The dominance hierarchy is maintained by fighting behavior, which in mice is highly ritualized and an important part of community life. Fighting serves not only to maintain community order but to solidify each individual's place within the community, preserving the sense of structure essential to such primitive little societies. Fighting patterns are innate in mice and are characteristic of the species worldwide. That they are innate and not learned is shown by the various breeds of mice that have been developed under domestication and show variants of the standard ritual in accordance with the desires of their breeders.

Fighting begins when previously unacquainted male house mice meet and begin a ritual of mutual grooming, which gradually becomes rougher and rougher until one of the participants may attempt to mount the other as if for sex. Ultimately one of the pair begins to fight, at which point the interaction becomes a biting, clawing brawl of two. When a mouse is defeated it either flees or, rarely, offers its belly to its attacker in a gesture of submission. Because the response to such appeasement behavior is not well-developed in mice, the attacker may continue his aggression until the loser leaves the community territory. A fleeing male mouse in itself is invitation for pursuit, and fleeing and fighting may continue for some time after one participant displays submission.

Fighting in male mice is initially induced by the hormone testosterone, which is identical to that causing young human males to fight and drive noisy cars fast in the night. However, after fighting behavior has established itself in a young male mouse, even castration will not end it. Fighting improves with experience, and dominance in the community hierarchy is acquired through many fights and must perpetually be defended. Although females are not part of dominance fighting, a female in milk is often aggressive to males, who usually submit to her attack. Young mice squeal and squirm when touched but after a week or so raise their paws in a characteristic defense gesture that is respected by their elders. Within the mouse community all eating places, escape holes, urination and defecation areas, and storage burrows are held in common. All adult members of a community are given to bouts of community grooming, which helps free them of parasites and serves to increase recognition among individuals and solidify the family bond.

If, through a fortunate combination of absence of predation and availability of food, a community becomes too large for its territory, groups of young mice break off in search of new space. A mated female usually founds a colony by dropping her litter in a suitable place for burrows, and another community grows in the earth like the roots of a plant. If for some reason no additional territory is available and population pressure continues, adolescent females become infertile. Their vaginas remain closed, the uterus becomes thin, and the ovaries discontinue their activity. Hormonal changes in mice resulting from overcrowding produce group restlessness and social disintegration, resulting in an increase in fighting behavior. Wounds weaken the health of many mice, who succumb to disease or are driven out, and through a variety of discontinuities the community population is restored to optimal level.

Like all murids, the house mouse is subject to intense predation by mammals, birds, reptiles, and even fish and large insects. To offset its losses, the house mouse is incredibly fecund. With a gestation period of twenty-one days, females produce litters of from six to thirteen young. If no male mouse is present the females tend to come into estrus only rarely, but introduction of a male causes simultaneous heat in the females of a colony. This response has been shown to be largely olfactory in nature; if the olfactory nerve is cut, females do not come into heat in response to the presence of a male. The estrus response to male mice is sometimes so strong that a pregnant female exposed to a stranger male may abort her young and come rapidly into heat.

Female mice may be impregnated while nursing young, in which case the length of the gestation period may lengthen a few days as she divides her energy between the litters born and unborn. Young mice are raised in the familiar mouse nest of shredded paper and other such vegetable matter, tucked away in some secure place. Baby mice may be brought up successfully at temperatures as low as 10 degrees Centigrade (50 degrees Fahrenheit) and have often been found alive in ice houses, occasionally in cavities gnawed into frozen meat itself. The young are blind and helpless at birth and their endothermic systems are not yet functional—they remain essentially the same temperature as their surroundings, as do reptiles, for several days after birth.

The eyes of baby mice open at thirteen days, and they begin eating solid foods at seventeen days, even though they may continue to nurse for up to a month. By the time they are eating solids with any regularity the young will have followed their mother from the nest on short excursions. They learn by imitation the boundaries of the community territory, the places for eating, feeding, defecating *et al.,* and gradually separate from their mother and join the adult group.

In the wild any predator larger than a praying mantis will cheerfully eat mice, and of a litter of ten mice only one or two normally reach maturity. Young in a litter that are disturbed by predators or stranger mice may be killed and eaten by the mother, or she may move the nest and accidentally kill some of the young in the process. Stability of the nesting area is of primary importance in the successful raising of young mice, and when the first storehouses of food appeared around permanent human settlements at the end of the last glacial period, there was strong selective pressure on mice to take advantage of these relatively safe and stable situations.

During those times there were several species of mice that might have profited from the invention of agriculture, but the central and western Asian house mouse subspecies *Mus musculus wagneri* appears to have been the most aggressive in invading and defending the nooks and crannies of human settlements. In the dry grasslands of its original habitat, *M. m. wagneri* had already evolved a number of physiological adaptations that permitted it to survive indefinitely on a grain diet that includes no liquid water. A gram of the carbohydrates that make up most of the grains on which house mice feed yields .6 gram of water while undergoing metabolic oxidation within the mouse's little body; this water is then utilized by the mouse as drinking water. To conserve this meager source of water in dry situations, mice have evolved several supporting physiological mechanisms. Unlike most mammals, which cool themselves by evaporation of water from respiratory surfaces and the skin, mice use their long bare tails as cooling surfaces. Although no water is lost through the tail, its uninsulated surface permits the transmission of excess heat to the surrounding air much as a radiator does in a house. When the surroundings become too cool and body temperature drops, the structure of blood vessels at the base of the tail permits reduction of the blood flow at that point, sharply reducing heat loss through the skin of the tail. In this respect the hairless tails of murids are evocative of the fins of *Dimetrodon* and other primitive experimenters with endothermy, in that to a certain extent murids still rely on their surrounding temperature to maintain the proper body heat.

Another adaptation aiding the house mouse in its invasion of artificial habitats was its burrow, which serves as a sort of extrabodily physiological mechanism for the conservation of water. These burrows are so constructed as to maintain a high rate of humidity in even the driest situations, their air being kept near the point of saturation at all times thanks to escaping moisture in the breath of the inhabitants. House mice spend much of their time in their burrows and often pack stuffing into drafty places, so that for much of its day any individual mouse is in a situation where evaporative body-water loss is at a minimum. In buildings, there is often little opportunity for actual burrowing, but mice in such places counter by constructing nests that are carefully insulated to maintain an internal humidity largely independent of that on the outside.

In order to rid itself of the poisonous wastes of metabolism, an animal must dissolve them in water and pass them to the outside of its system. The excretion of wastes—urination—therefore represents a certain amount of water loss, and in mice a number of modifications are present to minimize this loss. The kidneys of house mice are amazingly efficient; when water must be conserved, these organs may return most of the water used in the filtering process to the body, while producing urine that reaches a concentration in salts of up to four times that of seawater. Because of this a house mouse is one of the few mammals that can drink seawater and remain alive for any length of time. Then again, female mammals are of course subject to a significant water loss in the process of nursing their young. The milk of a lactating female mouse is often as fatty as that of whales and other mammals inhabiting regions where fresh drinking water is not available. This milk consequently contains less water per unit volume than that of most mammals, and the nursing house mouse is subjected to far less water loss than would otherwise be the case.

Mice sharply alter their diets in response to different conditions of water availability. As we have noted, the carbohydrate content of dry seeds will produce water in the mouse's body, and thus a mouse can survive on a diet of dry seeds (which in addition are actually about 10 percent water at their driest) with no liquid water. However, in situations where a high-fat or protein meal is the only one available, mice must obtain liquid water. The processing of proteins and fats by the body requires more water than it produces, and the urea from protein breakdown must be accompanied by more water in excretion. Mice eating such diets without a ready supply of drinking water will reduce their intake of food as much as possible to conserve water. In natural situations insects are usually available, and in dry times up to 90 percent of a mouse's diet may be insects, largely for the water they contain. A mouse in a dry environment may lose up to 40 percent of its body weight in water and still be able to recover rapidly when water becomes available again.

Finally, house mice are able to slip into a stress-induced torpor if their body water level falls too low. This condition of unconsciousness and reduced metabolic activity permits a storing of resources until such time as water is again available, at which point the mouse resumes normal activity. A mouse in such a torpor is actually in a state of defensive hibernation, sometimes for as long as several days, from which it emerges either spontaneously or when disturbed. In this way a house mouse *in extremis* from water loss may simply wait out its problems in a deep sleep.

It is not difficult to see that a granary or house, with its carefully maintained dryness and warmth, is the ideal setting for such aridity-adapted little animals as house mice. With the complex of water-conservation mechanisms discussed above, immense numbers of mice may breed in granaries, whose human builders carefully create dry microclimates to preserve their contents, and in which liquid water is for all practical purposes nonexistent. In one such granary *eight tons* of mice were killed in a rodent eradication program lasting only four nights, a tribute in blood to the efficiency of the animals' water-conservation physiology.

Having invaded the first buildings of early agricultural humans, *Mus musculus wagneri* quickly subspeciated into a number of new races, each adapted to one of the foreign climates to which men and mice have moved in the intervening millennia. *Mus musculus spicilegus* and *M. m. bactrianus* appeared among early farming settlements of southwestern Asia, and from one of these races descend the northern European subspecies, *M. m. domesticus* and *M. m. musculus,* and the Mediterranean subspecies, *M. m. brevirostris*. Some taxonomists claim racial status for up to sixteen natural strains of house mice around the world, basing their assertions on color, size, and other characteristics that quickly change when populations of the little animals are seeded in new habitats by their human landlords. The house mouse as a species is perpetually changing, and the field for rodent taxonomists is wide open for decades to come.

The small size (usually fewer than 20 grams) of adult house mice is their greatest advantage in the twilight world of our mammalian inquilines. The larger murid inquilines, our two species of "house rats," are both stronger and more aggressive than house mice, but they are also more easily noticed by humans or their carnivorous satellites, the dogs and cats, and are thus greatly restricted in activity. House mice, however, can fit into astonishingly tight places with ease and comfort; an entire nest of living young mice and their mother has been found in the ice around a brine pipe in a fishing vessel. House mice specialize in quickness and silence, and through thousands of generations of vigorous selection at the hands of humanity, these rodents have come to resemble little bits of the night itself with their skill at moving about undetected.

It is likely that the first mice associated specifically with human activity took up residence in the earliest southwest Asian sedentary villages. Racks of drying meat and storehouses of vegetation were lucrative finds, and mice took to breeding in and around these convenient food sources. As time passed and humans began to domesticate mammals, food and droppings of domestic herbivores presented new sources of food, and outbuildings constructed to house these animals were, logically, mouse mansions. Because of their nocturnal and subterranean nature, house mice were easily able to adapt to the life between walls that was becoming increasingly available in the dawn of agriculture.

Traveling on ships and over the land trade routes of Neolithic and historical humanity, house mice quickly colonized Europe and the Far East. A basket or pot of grain can support an entire family of house mice with plenty of space and food, and in the dark holds of merchant ships laden with produce thousands of house mice might travel in comfort. Over land, in wagons and even in baggage carried on horses, mice found their way to fresh, unmoused countries throughout Eurasia and northern Africa. The author once found, on opening his pack in camp after a long day's hike through a mountain wilderness, that a mouse was hidden in his sleeping bag. This mouse scrambled off into the presumably mouseless alpine meadow and for all we know established a new high-mountain race of *M. musculus* for the edification of taxonomists of the future. It is in this very fashion that house mice have finally come to inhabit even the underground dormitories of humans living in the windswept wastes of Antarctica, and it was early in the mouse's career as inquiline that civilizations came to know him as a major competitor for the foods they so painstakingly produced. The house mouse became a threat to Man.

As an animal becomes part of human life, so it becomes part of human myth, and the mouse is no exception. Attempting to explain the origins of the hordes of mice that stole their food and infested their dwellings, people invented tales. The ancient Hebrews considered mice unclean things, perhaps sent by their peculiarly ferocious god to punish wayward humans. The Zoroastrians agreed, adding that the killing of mice was a service to humanity—quite true then as today. Ancient Egyptians believed that mice were spawned from the mud of the Nile in flood, and designed an entire species of carnivore, *Felis domesticus,* the house cat, from specifications provided by the house mouse.

The Greeks, noting that the numbers of mice increased in times of human health and prosperity, associated them with Apollo, patron of physicians. Mice were bred in Greek temples and their reproductive rate was regarded as auspicious when rapid. Mice became a symbol of delicacy in certain areas of life and were believed related to the cure of such disorders as constipation, snakebite, baldness, cataracts, and epilepsy. In drama the house mouse came to symbolize tenderness, "little mouse" being a common Greek term of endearment. A dramatic satire lampooning the *Iliad* was named the *Batrachomyomachy,* or "War of Frogs and Mice." In it the frog-king Physiognathos abducts the mouse princess Aricharpax, and, with full Homeric intervention of the gods and all, the war lasts an entire day. Aristotle believed mice to be spontaneously generated from dirt in houses and ships, while some of his contemporaries countered with the notion that mice were actually born of the interaction of decaying grain with light, a sort of mammalian photosynthesis!

The Roman Plautus suggested to his contemporaries in *Truculentus* that they "Consider the little mouse, how sagacious an animal it is which never entrusts its life to one hole only," and Pliny the Elder observed that "when a building is about to fall all the mice desert it."

Since classical times the mouse has been important in European myth and fable, but until recently almost no one understood the far more important part the little beasts play in carrying disease among humans, thus changing the history of civilization itself. In the first century B.C. the Greek geographer Strabo expressed a suspicion that mice were somehow related to certain epidemics, but his suggestion remained unnoticed until the invention of the microscope and the advent of scientific epidemiology. We now know that the house mouse is a vector of bubonic plague, rickettsial pox, salmonellosis, spotted fever, typhus, tularemia, and a host of lesser diseases that have plagued our kind for thousands of years.

It might therefore seem a quirk of evolutionary justice that house mice should be domesticated by us for use in combating disease. In classical times, as we have seen, mice were bred in temples and even kept as pets. There are records of white strains, indicating that the Greeks and Romans had spent many mouse generations selecting color variants from mutant specimens. However, it was not until modern times that true medical research began on a large scale, and with this intensified research came the need for an animal in which human physiologic response could be duplicated or nearly duplicated for experimental purposes. The perfect animal would be one that was quick of generation and short of life, and one whose responses to experiments were similar enough to those of a human subjected to the same conditions so that human physiology might be extrapolated from animal data. In the Orient, which has had house mice for as long as the West, mouse breeding was a hobby among the aristocracy and many novel strains had been developed over generations of selective breeding. American medical research went to Oriental breeders for mice, and in the early twentieth century *Mus musculus* in its domesticated form began arriving in medical laboratories across the nation.

Under the pressure of artificial selection, house mice have evolved some strange and sometimes disquieting forms. In research in cancer and radiation exposure, mice with no hair have been bred. Other cancer research has produced numerous strains with a predilection for a cancer of one sort or another. These monsters are so carefully bred that the very day of tumor appearance is estimable for the breed, so that individuals become walking cancer time bombs, dying at a time determined by their genes. Behavior is also largely genetically based in mice, and traits may be selected to produce special fighting or grooming traits, or lack of either of these behaviors. House mice with abnormalities of balance or neurological structure, epilepsy, and even higher than usual intelligence are available from a number of breeding laboratories worldwide.

It looks, then, as if mice are here with us to stay. There is no getting around them—they are as much a part of the human experience as dogs or cats or wheat or barley. With our other inquilines they mop up inefficiently managed food energy, waste in the artificial ecosystem. In that capacity they are a logical product of our activity, an accessory consumer of cultivated products. As representatives of primitive mammalian structure and behavior, house mice are interesting complements to the intricate and highly evolved human societies in which they take part. They seem to round us out in an odd way, and I for one would miss them if they disappeared. But they won't.

5 Rats

There is little doubt that some rat, and probably the brown rat (*Rattus norvegicus*), is actually the finest—in every sense of the word, and especially in efficiency—product that Nature has managed to create on this planet to date.

So says Ivan T. Sanderson in his classic *Living Mammals of the World,* and his speculation is well based; of all the hundreds of thousands of thousands of species of animals described by contemporary zoology, the murids of genus *Rattus* seem the most exuberantly successful, even in the face of centuries of concentrated conflict with humanity.

There are five hundred and fifty to five hundred and seventy currently recognized species of rats in genus *Rattus.* These are all small to medium-sized rodents with an ancient and perfected mammalian design over which is superimposed a learning ability and social structure unsurpassed in the rodent world. Two species, *Rattus rattus* and *Rattus norvegicus,* are responsible for most of the competition offered us humans, and these are the ones that you are most likely to encounter.

The first of these two species to join our ancestors is commonly known as the black, Alexandrian, or fruit rat, in spite of the facts that it is not usually black, not limited to Alexandria in distribution, and not specifically interested in fruit, as it eats anything at all. *Rattus rattus* is, however, fond of trees and the upper parts of buildings, and thus warrants its other nickname, roof rat, which we will use throughout this discussion. Roof rats seem to have originated in the warm, wet areas of southeast Asia, where they lived among the thick trees and shrubbery of lowland and coastal regions.

125

Their association with human beings goes back so far that its beginnings are lost in time, but they probably took to our company when the earliest permanent settlements of people began to appear in the area eight to ten millennia ago. Being larger and more conspicuous than house mice, roof rats were not as easily concealed in cargos and baggage, and their spread beyond their natural range had to await the advancement of human technology to a point where large and capacious seagoing vessels were first designed. For five millennia, sailing ships have passed to and fro along the southern and eastern coasts of Asia, carrying the fruits of the labors of a thousand peoples. Into these ships, inevitably, came the roof rats as well. From the thatched roofs of buildings overhanging the docks and canals of water-loving peoples, onto the rigging and up the painters and hawsers of vessels of trade and pleasure and war, the rats moved by night, by accident, by chance, to places where roof rats were never meant to be. From its original Indonesian home, *R. rattus* quickly spread to China, Japan, the Philippines, New Guinea, India, and, probably around the time of the emperor Constantine, the Middle East.

In these new climates the roof rats became obligate inquilines limited in range by the new climates to which they were introduced. House mice receded before the larger newcomers, pressed back into smaller holes. Even in lands where house cats had been domesticated, the rat encountered only sporadic resistance; a house cat kills only forty or fifty roof rats a year, far fewer than would dent the rats' stupendous reproductive capacity. In a human world dependent on grain, the roof rat flourished, sampling all the pleasures of the human table in addition to the grass-seed staples. Vegetables, meat, and even human sewage were consumed by the rats, who quickly overran any human community into which they were introduced. Spreading throughout the Orient, roof rats subspeciated in accordance with the requirements of new climates, until today we can distinguish about ten Oriental races, recognizable by differences in build and coloring.

It was probably with the rise of Islam that roof rats entered the Mediterranean and ultimately Europe. The jihads, holy wars of conversion conducted after the seventh century by Muslim warriors, brought Muhammedan hegemony, trade, and civilization to much of the Mediterranean world, while in the east and south the Muhammedans spread into India and along the coast of east Africa. Trade across the empire naturally passed roof rats from the coasts of the Indian Ocean to the eastern end of the Mediterranean, and eventually roof rat colonies were established along the north coast of Africa. The currently popular guess is that Europeans of the Crusades brought roof rats back with them in ships or in baggage, but all that is certain is that the rats were introduced to a few European ports sometime before A.D. 1095, when their presence is first definitely recorded.

Roof rats seem to have spread quickly once they were introduced to the European subcontinent, so that by A.D. 1284, according to the records, the German city of Hamelin was forced to employ an exterminator to rid its attics of the many roof rats living there. This exterminator was unable to collect his fee from the Bürgermeister of Hamelin, however, and his alleged marching of the town's children into the nearby mountain called the Koppenberg is the low point in that town's long history. At any rate, by the fourteenth century the roof rat was well enough established in Europe that rat-transmitted *Pasteurella pestis,* the organism causing bubonic plague, managed to kill some twenty-five million people, more than a quarter of the European population, during the Black Death.

Plague is a natural disease of wild rodents and rabbits, infecting many of them without causing noticeable damage. Infected populations of wild rodents are called reservoirs for the disease, which is transmitted from one to another by various species of rodent fleas. In Europe, plague has periodically broken out among the crowded peoples of that troubled area, who have lived in close conjunction with house mice for millennia. However, the roof rat, living as it does in attics and roofs of buildings and carrying a greater *per capita* population of fleas, was the rodent primarily responsible for the Black Death. Although the precise connection was not to be established for centuries, contemporary chroniclers remarked on a vast die-off of roof rats before the beginning of the plague, and similar die-offs were reported before each of the lesser subsequent epidemics of bubonic plague in Europe. As these rats died in the houses and work-places of humanity, their fleas left them and sometimes went to humans in their search for the proper host.

R. rattus made *P. pestis* a truly intimate part of European ecology and economics. In much of central Europe, ratcatchers acquired high professional status, and bounties were paid for dead rats presented to the authorities. In Frankfurt and other large towns, the Jews of the ghetto were taxed thousands of rat tails annually by the Christian Bürgermeisters. Dogs, and particularly cats, which had suffered a very low status in Europe for some centuries, became regarded as protective against the plague, even though the precise connection between the carnivores and the disease—predation on rats—was not suspected at the time. Indeed, plague was regarded by the people of that benighted age as a heavenly punishment, or the result of "corrupt vapors" emerging from swamps, ghettos, or even the stars. Papal records of the time speak of two hundred thousand European villages wiped out by the disease, which adjusted the genetics of the European population to such an extent that the collective immunity of Europeans may be greater today than in centuries past. This in itself is an indication that the connection between plague and humans is a recent one, unlike the long and healthy coexistence between plague and the wild animals in which it is endemic. Because roof rats are also killed by the plague, however, it seems that the disease was also recently introduced to that species, and that the centuries of plague in rats and humans represent a stage in which *P. pestis, R. rattus,* and *H. sapiens* were coevolving to a point where the bacteria might exist symbiotically with these mammalian species as they do in their wild hosts.

Plague has continued its activity in human populations to this day. It is believed to have been transmitted to North America by Chinese workers imported to San Francisco around the turn of the century, and a reservoir of the disease persists among wild and inquiline rodents in the mountain states of the American West. As recently as 1892–98 some eleven million natives of India were stricken with plague, and lesser epidemics have surfaced sporadically around the world—wherever there are humans, rats, and fleas. However, the invention of antibiotics such as tetracycline have relegated plague to the position of a minor infection if caught in time, and it looks as if the further coevolution of *pestis* with *sapiens* must await a time when antibiotics are not readily available, or when *pestis* circumvents the action of antibiotics with a new, resistant strain.

Also in medieval times, another rat-carried disease assaulted the peoples of Europe. Typhus, caused by a minuscule parasitic coccobacillus called *Rickettsia prowazekii,* is only one of a number of diseases which are called by the medical profession the Rickettsia group. All of these are transmitted by arthropods, and there is cause to believe that *Rickettsia* and its relatives originally evolved somewhere in the systems of these small animals where no real harm was done to them. This would have occurred long before the evolution of mammals, but when mammals appeared, and with them certain arthropods specialized to parasitize them, the first transmission of *Rickettsiae* to mammals probably took place.

Among the *Rickettsia* diseases infecting humans are South African and Siberian tick-bite fevers, Boutonneuse fever, trench or Volhynian fever, Rocky Mountain spotted fever, Japanese river valley disease, Rumanian tick fever, and, of course, typhus. It is likely that typhus first broke out in Europe when a human body louse, *Pediculus humanus,* accidentally bit a roof rat harboring some *Rickettsiae.* This louse realized its error too late, and even as it returned to its human host it was dying of typhus. It is usu-

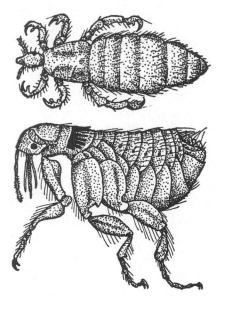

Two vectors of disease between rats and humans.
Top, the human body louse; *bottom*, the rat flea.

ally the case that the human body louse dies of typhus more often than the human to whom it passes the disease. The fact that all the *Rickettsiae* infecting the louse die also, except for the few that may be passed on to a human, is an indication that infecting human body lice is not the proper business of *Rickettsiae* at all. We can assume therefore that typhus is an accidental infection of humans in a cycle that normally transmits the parasites to wild rodents by arthropod-power. Rodents involved are normally only slightly affected by the *Rickettsiae,* to which they have developed a tolerance over millions of years of coevolution. But when an accidental transmission to an animal not normally part of the cycle occurs, the parasite may cause a violent reaction on the part of the new host, and this reaction we see as a disease.

The first case of European typhus of which we are certain is recorded in A.D. 1083, but it was not until 1546 that a precise clinical description of the disease appears in *De Contagione,* a volume of medical lore prepared by the physician Fracastorius. Typhus begins its course with an influenza-like fever accompanied by intermittent chills and often a deep depression. Rash begins to appear on the shoulders and back, gradually spreading down the extremities and even to the palms of the hands and soles of the feet.

This rash begins as masses of pink spots, which gradually turn purplish and then red-brown as the disease progresses. The most painful symptom of typhus is a severe headache, and it is from descriptions of this symptom alone that we are sometimes able to deduce an incidence of typhus from an old chronicle.

Until recent years there were precious few bathtubs in European civilization, and lice were pretty much a way of life. The body of Thomas à Becket is said to have leaked parasites from its vestments for some days after his murder, and the custom of shaving the head and wearing a periwig is likely to have been a counter to lousiness. Throughout the world, wherever Europeans congregated, there were strictures of etiquette relating to proper moments for the killing of lice about one's person; George Washington recorded at age fourteen a "rule of etiquette" to the effect that a gentleman should "kill no vermin, as Fleas, lice, tics, etc., in the sight of others, if you See any filth or thick Spittle, put your foot Dexteriously upon it; if it be upon the Cloth of your Companion, put it off privately, and if it be upon your own Cloths, return thanks to him who puts it off." The densely populated European civilization, containing tons of lice, was like a trap set to catch *Rickettsiae* when the roof rats first wandered in.

The first typhus epidemics had been raging across Europe for some centuries before the Europeans began their famous raging across the planet. The human body louse is as universally distributed as its host, and Europeans, accompanied by *Rickettsiae*-infected rats in their luggage and ships, quickly spread typhus among the lice and peoples of the lands they overran. In Mexico the dominant civilization at the time of the European conquest was the Aztec theocracy. Evolving in a land where there were few large mammalian herbivores remaining to provide its citizens with protein, this civilization relied on maize and beans together to provide the dense, poor population with all the amino acids necessary for health. However, like all crops, beans and maize are not always predictable at harvest time, and there is evidence that the Aztec priests were forced to adopt a state-managed cannibalistic protein ecology to support their minions. Human prisoners were levied by thousands from outlying subject states, the victims usually being ritualistically fattened before being sacrificed and eaten by celebrants in the many festivals of the Aztec year. Although Spanish writers at the time of the Conquest viewed the sanguinary religion of the Aztecs as an institution of the Devil, current research indicates that the fierce gods of this brilliant people were actually a cultural adaptation to the unique ecological problems posed by dense populations of humans with no large domesticated food animals.

Among the poorest Aztecs, composing most of the population, it was customary to collect one's lice as a personal sacrifice to the noble priests. Lice are protein literally drawn from one's body, composed of oneself, and the presentation of bags of lice was a symbolic act of self-sacrifice worthy of the most devoted subject. The lice of Aztecs and other Americans quickly picked up typhus from Spanish rats, and the destruction of the Mexican civilization proceeded smoothly as more than half of the indigenous population died in epidemic after epidemic of the disease.

In recent decades, with the advent of typhus vaccination and the bathtub, typhus has been reduced to a rarity among the richer peoples of the world. Even so, an occasional case is spotted in the most advanced of nations. A small epidemic of typhus in a New York hospital was correctly diagnosed only when a doctor visiting from the Soviet Union, where there are plenty of lice (some three million Russians died of typhus after the October Revolution), recognized the symptoms of the disease in the New Yorkers.

Roof rats, however, are still very much with us. In the spread of Europeans across the oceans of the world, these rats made their own bid for world empire. Because of their inability to tolerate cool climates, the range of roof rats in colder countries is limited to the artificial microhabitats built by humans. In warmer climates, however, roof rats quickly move into the surrounding countryside wherever they reach land. Being an arboreal creature that never burrows, the roof rat is limited to the higher parts of buildings and other structures, and generations may live there without ever descending to earth. Indeed, in some warmer parts of the United States, roof rats have adopted arboreal niches nearly identical to those of urban squirrels in cooler places. These rats are the so-called bald-tailed squirrels of southern California and the Gulf Coast palm trees.

The roof rat is a graceful, slender creature beautifully designed for leaping about in trees and other high places, The rat's balance is well developed and its bare tail is partly prehensile, longer than the entire body, and sometimes serving as a sort of fifth leg as the animal tightropes across cables and wires. The eyes of roof rats are proportionately large, as a climbing animal must often rely on sight in judging distances. Even if a fall should occur, the roof rat is able to flatten itself to increase air resistance, sometimes surviving falls as long as 20 meters.

The hegemony of the roof rat on the European continent was to last only a few centuries, however, for a close relative from the arid steppes of central and northern Asia was already on the move toward the West. This was *Rattus norvegicus,* the Norway, brown, gray, sewer, water, house, or wharf rat, "wanderratte," whose color may be any from black to white, whose land of origin is not Norway, and who lives anywhere it can find enough of a human economic system in which to conceal itself. More than it deserves the more common common name Norway rat or brown rat, *R. norvegicus* probably deserves the antique and colorful British name "wanderratte," and it is this name that we will use here.

It seems likely in retrospect that the wanderratte traveled from its native home in and about Mongolia with the hordes of humans who also left those parts during medieval times under pressure from famine, epidemics, and the Empire of China. At any rate, there is some evidence that the first wanderrattes to have reached Europe did so in the company of migrating Mongols and, later, Slavonic peoples whose original homeland was overrun by Mongols. The first definite European record of wanderrattes dates from A.D. 1727, a good "mouse year" throughout the continent, in which millions of wanderrattes were seen swimming the Volga near its Caspian delta at Astrakhan. Thence the hordes of rats seem to have spread westward through the Ukraine, southern Poland, and Bohemia, probably aided by the ships and wagons and incessant wars of humans. Oddly, one of the first European nations reached by wanderrattes was England, in which *R. norvegicus* was reported as early as 1728. This invasion of Britannic biological sovereignty was a direct result of the advanced and wealthy British maritime technology, which also was to bring Empire to that sanguinary people. In 1740 an "army" of wanderrattes invaded East Prussia, and by 1750 the new rodents were common throughout all the little Prussian principalities. Wanderrattes traveled a lot by ship, and it was while disembarking from Norwegian vessels in Great Britain and America that they acquired the misnomer "Norway rat," which has stuck with them even in their scientific name to this day. By 1775 wanderrattes were firmly established in England's American colonies, and less than a century later they accompanied other Europeans in the settling of California, being reported there as early as 1851.

The success of *R. norvegicus* is based in large part on its fossorial, or burrowing, habits. These rats were originally inhabitants of arid, cold places, where they constructed, and often maintained for generations, elaborate systems of underground burrows connected by concealed surface runways. The wanderratte is larger, stronger, and more aggressive than its arboreal cousin the roof rat, and when introduced to Europe began a process of eradicating the established species to a point where roof rats now inhabit only certain coastal cities and, of course, ships, having given up the inland to their fierce relatives. Wanderrattes first invaded the basements and sewage systems of European cities, rising higher in the architecture as their populations rose, until the roof rats were chased from the roofs and evicted.

It is possible that the reduced modern occurrence of plague and typhus and other rat-borne diseases is a direct result of the displacement of roof rats by wanderrattes over much of the civilized world. Living as they do in the upper parts of buildings, roof rats tend to release their arthropod parasites into the human population when they die, whereas wanderrattes, which prefer the darker, moister places in basements and sewers beneath the habitats of humans, seem simply to lose many of their parasites at death to the earth, to water, and to the general inclemency of their habitat. Such parasites are ill equipped to make the ascent to the living areas of the humans above them. In some areas populations of each species share a single structure, roof rats in the roof and wanderrattes in the basement, but through most of their old range the roof rats have been extirpated and wanderrattes reign unchallenged. Still, roof rats constitute an estimated 90 percent of any shipboard population of rats today and can survive comfortably at high temperatures that might kill wanderrattes.

Wanderrattes usually range through various shades of gray and brown. Unlike the roof rat, *R. norvegicus* possesses a tail that is shorter than its body and eyes and ears that are in smaller proportion to its head than those of the roof rat. The heavy, blunt snout of the wanderratte also offers a sharp contrast to the slender nose of the roof rat. As in the case of other murids, there is a variety of recognized subspecies of wanderrattes, distinguishable by color and migratory history, but the species is so new in its relationships to humanity that these subspecies are at best debatable and we won't bother ourselves with them. In any event the human world is assured a population of rat-sized inquilines no matter where its earthly wanderings take it.

Incidentally, "rat-sized" is a term that bears some inspection. From such cities as New York, whose inhabitants are always willing (with justifiable pride) to relate amazing tales of their inquilines, come stories of "rats as big as spaniels" and "the superrats of the South Bronx, big as cats an' twice as mean," and other creatures of television, newspaper, and cinema. While it is certain that the population of *R. norvegicus* in New York and other modern cities is made of tough stuff to survive in such adverse environments, the *very* largest recorded individual of the species weighed only 650 grams, somewhat more than a pound (house cats weigh about 10 pounds), its length from tip of nose to tip of tail being 474 millimeters or about 19 inches. It must be noted that this was a domestic specimen specially raised for size, and that it grossly exceeded in mass and length any wild wanderratte ever recorded. Indeed, the huge animal was so poorly designed that it could barely move about, a far cry from the lithe wild rats of the city. The upper limits for wild *R. norvegicus* are some 480 grams in weight and about 460 millimeters in length, while these limits in roof rats are 340 grams and 450 millimeters respectively. Such sizes are optimal for inquilines; a larger animal would be simply too conspicuous and would experience sharp selective pressure toward smaller size. It is possible that, were there no house mice, populations of smaller rats might appear to fill that lucrative niche, but selective pressure against any size increase is too strong in creatures of dark and narrow places. Still, there just *might,* somewhere out in the wide world of our inquiline rats, be some unfortunate mutant the size of a *small* grown cat, and the author here requests that anyone collecting such an animal send at least its skull and skin to a zoologist at any accredited institution of higher learning to set the record straight. In the meantime newsmen and other aficionados of giant rats might consume a six-pack of Turkey Buzzard Malt Liquor as fast as they can before venturing to the South Bronx. Taken as prescribed, this will permit their seeing large numbers of weighty rats of many pleasing colors.

In different parts of the world, notably Asia, the center of murid evolution, other rats have occupied the niches offered by human activity to animals of the general rat size. When the ancestors of Polynesian voyagers began their oceanic wanderings from southeast Asia, they carried in their canoes a self-replicating food supply in the form of the little rat *Rattus exulans,* which may have profoundly altered the prehistoric ecologies of thousands of islands to which it was introduced. More recently, the migrations of the starving millions of India from rural villages to the new urban complexes have provided a niche for the indigenous Bengal rat, *Bandicota bengalensis,* a murid closely related to genus *Rattus.* But the early successes of *R. rattus* and *R. norvegicus* have assured these two species dominance of the rate niche on a worldwide basis, and it is these that we usually mean when we discuss rats.

Their small size, their generalized structure, exhibiting little or no specialization to any narrow way of life, and their omnivorous diet are all factors contributing to the ascendance of inquiline rats; but the primary source of their present status is the structure of their societies, permitting the exchange and retention of experience between generations in a tribe. This passing on of information within a community is a form of tradition, the use of which is the chief ingredient in the success formulas of both rats and their human landlords.

Other murid inquilines.
Top: the little rat *R. exulans;*
bottom: the Bengal rat,
Bandicota bengalensis.

In natural situations, that is to say, in the sewers of Chicago or the granaries of New Orleans, rats live in families that are normally descended from a single pair. Families are founded when rats invade a previously rat-free habitat, and a male and female establish a territory, which they begin to hold against other rats by fighting. Fighting behavior within species of rats is highly ritualized, consisting of a ceremonial display followed by actual attack, and normally occurs only in defense of territory against out-group rats. On sighting an intruder, a rat clacks its incisors, arches its back, and erects body hairs to appear larger. Broadside, it approaches the intruder while urinating and defecating and mincing about on stiffly extended legs. This ritual usually serves to chase the intruder away, and actual contact between strangers is rare. It also permits the home rat to size up its opponent; if the intruder is much larger than the attacking defender, the

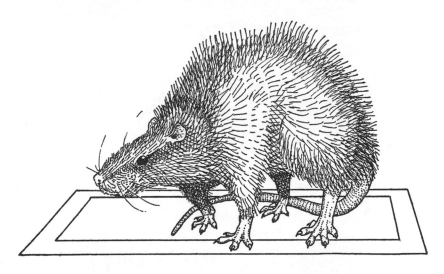

Rat in threat stance, attempting to appear as large
and fearsome as possible.

ritual is prolonged and intensified, while if the intruder is a little squeaky
runt, the defender may dispense with some of the ritual and attack outright.

If an intruding rat is somehow prevented from immediate retreat, the
defender springs at him and strikes rapidly and repeatedly with the sturdy
front paws while biting with the teeth. Although a rat's gnawing equipment
is formidable, these bites usually do not harm an opponent nearly as much
as the psychological stress caused by being out of one's own territory and in
the territory of a strange family of rats. Prevented from retiring, an intruder rat quickly succumbs to a form of shock culminated by cardiac
arrest. Thus the genetic integrity of rat families may be maintained over
generations, such that some astonishingly small populations or tribes develop a characteristic coloring or a behavioral trait or even a resistance to
a specific poison. If such traits confer on their possessors a marked advantage in the exploitation of human resources, they may permit the growth
of this particular population until it becomes the exclusive rat inhabitant of
an area and achieves subspecies status in the annals of rodent taxonomy.
The usual difference of opinion between taxonomists as to whether a group
does or does not constitute a subspecies indicates that taxonomy is still a
science of human error and subjectivity; however, briefly, a *species* is composed of a set of organisms capable of interbreeding to produce fertile offspring, while a subspecies or race is composed of those members of a

species exhibiting (in the eye of the taxonomist) characteristics distinguishing them from their conspecifics at large. A strain is an incipient subspecies, and a breed is a strain constructed through artificial selection by human agency.

Once a pair of adult rats has established a territory, of course, they mate. If she is not in estrus, and she never is until she inhabits an established territory, the female will strike at the male with her hind legs should he wax amorous. Once she comes into heat, however, the same female will copulate from two hundred to five hundred times during that estrus period. Thoroughly mated, the female builds a nest, which may vary somewhat from situation to situation but is usually constructed of soft insulating materials such as straw, cloth, and the like; and after a gestation period of from twenty-two to twenty-four days, wrinkled pink young are born blind and helpless. After throwing a litter of from six to twelve young, the female may mate again within forty-eight hours, whelping up to seven litters per year. Young rats reach sexual maturity in about three months, with the end result that a single pair of rats can theoretically be responsible for offspring totaling fifteen hundred in a single year. Thus if even one pregnant mutant rat survives a poisoning or other purge, she can quickly rebuild a population equipped with this new resistance.

The female licks her young all over at birth in a reflex action that stimulates their elimination behavior. If this licking does not occur, a situation found only in rat tribes suffering from a stress such as population overload, the young rats quickly die. This is an inherited pattern that serves to reduce pressure on disturbed families—a sort of built-in infanticide permitting energy use by the experienced adults so essential to the well-being of the tribe.

Female rats defend their young actively and show the strong maternal devotion characteristic of mammals. Young rats falling out of the nest are retrieved by the mother, who recognizes them by various factors, such as odor and appearance. In tribes where more than one mother is lactating, females may share the task of raising young. In addition, females in milk adopt orphaned young rats. In the middle of their third week young rats begin to take solid food and by the fourth and fifth weeks are leaving their mothers to forage as adults. In this fashion tribes may grow in size to as large as two hundred members but usually number from ten to fifty.

The rat tribe is a generally amicable society of near-equals that do not recognize one another personally but by a tribe-membership pheromone (an odorous information-transmitting chemical produced by individuals of the tribe). At food or water young rats are treated with indulgence, to the point where they are permitted to shoulder adults aside. Furthermore, the young rats in a healthy tribe are not denied access to females by the alpha, or dominant, males that form the core of the family. There is no pair bonding among rats, so genes are mixed joyously throughout the tribe.

These simple, affable societies inhabit territories that are actively defended from out-groupers, that is, rats from other tribes. Roof rats defend the family tree or building and all of the area traversed by tribe runways. Wanderrattes defend the tribe complex of burrows, which may be very extensive in an old family, and certain runways that are carefully marked with the tribe pheromone at every opportunity. Beyond the defended territory is the larger activity area, in which food is foraged and stranger rats are not attacked. In cities and other places densely populated with rats, the activity area is a roughly circular area of about 40 or 50 meters in diameter, through which the rats move largely by their senses of touch and smell. Because they do most of their moving in the dark, rats are equipped with highly sensitive vibrissae, or long whiskers, and thus tend to move along walls or other objects with which the vibrissae are perpetually in contact.

Because the activity area must produce the food to maintain the whole tribe, the members of that tribe are designed to be highly exploratory in nature, restless in their movements, and motivated by intense curiosity, so that they collectively leave no stone unturned. The general habit is to carry food back to the burrows or nest, where it may be stored or eaten in safety. Large pieces of food may be retrieved by several rats together, and groups of rats may attack other small animals for food, although they rarely act in real unison.

With regard to unfamiliar food, however, rats have evolved through their old battles with their human landlords an intense neophobia (fear of the new); they will leave the most inviting culinary delicacies alone for extended periods of time and will sample them only in tiny amounts when they first touch them. A result of the selective pressure exerted on rats by centuries of human trapping and poisoning, this neophobia is, in a way, a sort of perverse artifact created by human beings. It is because of this trait that rats are usually able to avoid the most cleverly concealed poisons and traps. In addition, information about any poisoned or otherwise injured tribe member is passed by means of a distress pheromone spread through the community and retained in the tribal memory, so that the group as a whole learns to avoid similar situations in the future.

Rats have also evolved great powers of discrimination in choosing their foods for nutritional content. Offered different varieties of food, both roof rats and wanderrattes select diets that are balanced and appropriate to the needs of the individual. Too, rats are able to locate minerals important to their metabolic processes from a variety of sources, even in the city. Information about these sources is probably transmitted through the tribe and retained for generations.

Although these are ancient and invariable behavioral patterns in healthy tribes of rats, in those tribes experiencing stresses caused by population increase a number of factors come into play to disperse the tribe and to reduce population to a point where the area of activity can support it healthily. Chief among these is a breakdown in social structure, in which stress is manifested by increased irritability on the part of the tribe's alpha males and by restlessness of the community as a whole. Youngsters, treated less tolerantly than before, are forced to forage on the periphery of the activity area, where they may fall to predators or be attacked by out-group rats. Often some of the young are actively driven out to search for another vacant habitat or to die among the out-group tribes. In addition, female rats in overpopulated tribes tend to skip estrus, and mothers disturbed by the pressure of numbers will frequently slay their young in response. The pituitary-adrenocortical system in mammals is affected by population stress, and it seems likely that increased group restlessness kills many subordinate animals through hyperstimulation of this system.

Through the centuries of their association with humans, rats have enjoyed a reputation for being vicious, cunning brutes motivated by an evil loathing of the good works of humanity. In song and legend, rats symbolize all that is base and destructive, and the epithet "dirty rat," with its connotation of craven underhandedness and a practically Nixonian disregard for all that is decent and tasteful, is an insult too popular to be regarded as accidental. This horror of rats is the natural outcome of their competition with us, for it cannot be said that these efficient inquilines operate for the benefit of civilization. However, the methods employed by rats in their exploitation of the human environment are sometimes strikingly similar to the methods employed by humans in their exploitation of the planetary surface at large. This similarity is recognized by peoples at war, who traditionally refer to out-group opponents as Hun rats, Nip rats, li'l gook rats, or arrogant bourgeois parasite rats.

Humans fling these names about even as they join their opponents in perpetrating outrage after outrage on humanity itself—rather in the fashion of stressed populations of rats.

But rats spend a good deal of time honestly earning the hatred of their human landlords. Initially both species of rats associated with humans for their stores of food; a single wanderratte can consume 20 to 25 kilograms (44 to 55 pounds) of grain per year, and what they do not consume they contaminate with urine and feces. In cases where rat management was not all it could be, rats have been found to have contaminated 95 percent of the maize in terminal facilities for export. In a recent survey 43 percent of all the grain storage facilities in the American heartland were found to be infested with rats. In another case more than 500,000 kilograms (over a million pounds) of sugar awaiting distribution to retail outlets was contaminated with rat urine. In addition, rats attack seeds and bulbs of ornamental and other plants; they pull young shoots and burrow about the roots of trees. In orchards roof rats are a particular nuisance, often sampling pieces of fruit, so that many are damaged but few actually eaten. In fields of sugarcane the rats are fond of taking just a little nibble at the base of each stalk, permitting the entrance of a fungus that kills the cane.

Rats are also capable of exploiting a food source of significantly higher quality than mere grain. Domestic birds, including ducks, chickens, geese, pigeons, and young turkeys, are attacked by rats, which sometimes eat the birds alive or leave them wounded and still living. Young piglets, lambs, and newborn calves are sometimes attacked by groups of rats, which also gnaw large holes in adult swine confined to pens too small for self-defense. Wanderrattes in particular are adapted to living around and in water, and in fish hatcheries they compete with the fish for food tossed into the water by the humans who run these places. Hatchery rats may also supplement their fish-food diet by attacking the fingerling fish themselves. Rats are a problem around zoos, where they compete with the inmates for food and transmit disease among captive animals with little resistance to infection. Sometimes rats even attack zoo specimens; in the Hagenbeck Tiergarten (Zoo) three elephants had to be killed after rats gnawed away the soft parts of their feet.

Humans sometimes maintain game populations in the wild, which are slaughtered by human hunters for the sake of amusement. Rats often compete with these hunters for wildlife, attacking game birds on the nest and destroying their young. In addition, the eggs of no species of bird save the largest and fiercest are safe from rats.

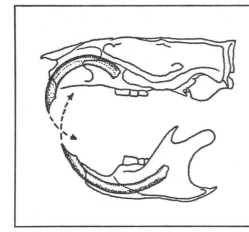

The incisors of rats, showing their circular growth and wear pattern.

As we noted previously, murid rats possess a body structure remarkable for its generalization and agility. Experiments with rat capabilities show us that a rat can jump horizontally up to 1.3 meters on a flat surface and can make a vertical jump of up to a meter. Rats regularly jump from heights as great as 5 meters, often traveling 3 meters horizontally as they fall. An adult rat can stretch about 45 centimeters horizontally or vertically from a standing point, and can squirm through any opening larger than a centimeter square. Rats shinny up vertical wires or ropes with ease and climb the outside of vertical pipes of up to 7 centimeters in diameter.

With their unequalled gnawing prowess, rats can perform feats of chewing that alter the human environment more than the activities of any other nonhuman animal. The pressure exerted by the incisor teeth of a wanderratte may equal 3000 kilograms per square centimeter, enabling rats to gnaw through pipes, bricks, cinderblocks, thin sheet steel, asphalt, and concrete. As the teeth of a rat grow some 13 centimeters per year, constant gnawing is necessary to keep these extraordinary implements short enough for movement. It is not uncommon to find a rat with one incisor that has been chipped, so that there is no grinding surface against which its opposite may wear away; the opposite tooth consequently grows out and around the animal's snout, ultimately piercing its skull if starvation does not kill it first. Perpetually gnawing, rats cause countless fires by piercing the insulation of electrical wires and chewing on the heads of kitchen matches. The chewing of wires also causes blackouts, some of them widespread, in some of the world's largest cities.

Burrowing by rats is a major cause of damage to building foundations, roadbeds, sidewalks, and earthworks such as dams and levees. In many cases rat burrows initiate erosion as rain washes away the earth of their walls. "Sanitary" landfills often serve as home to immense populations of rats, who burrow ever deeper into the nutritious hearts of the landfills, living in their dinner, assured of abundant food for generations of population expansion to come—until the food gives out, when millions of rats may emerge from the earth to search for more.

It is when the food gives out—when population strains at environmental limits and the tribe of rats is afflicted with hunger and discord—that rats meet humans face to face. A rat seen on the move in daylight, or in an exposed place at night, is a peripheral rat from a stressed tribe, an accidental, pressed by hunger and fear. It is from chance encounters with such animals that the reputation of rats for ferocity to humans is derived; a normal rat will do anything in its power to avoid the company of humans.

Living as intimately as they do with rats, humans are perpetually being bitten by fear-crazed rats; some ten in every one hundred thousand urban Americans report such bites annually. In large American cities several thousand individuals are bitten each year. Most of these are children who corner or approach rats, which then "fight like cornered rats," sometimes springing directly at the face. In the terrible wastes of the nation's ghettos, expanding populations of rats sometimes attack sleeping infants in their cribs, and even adults who are crippled or aged may be subjected to these attacks. However, these incidents ultimately say less about rats than they do about humans. The very existence of such helpless people in an environment where the rat population is permitted to grow so bloated makes a poignant testimony to the sorry state of any sense of ecological responsibility in twentieth-century *Homo sapiens*. The number of rats per human inhabitant of a political district is a direct measure of the efficiency of human enterprise in that district, and ecologically aware voters might someday tailor their votes to the inquiline population associated with the administration in power, a far more accurate gauge of political performance than the propaganda of politicians themselves!

On the other side, however, it cannot be denied that rats have prevented more human suffering than perhaps any other animal. Used as experimental animals in scientific research, rats provide an elegant model against which human responses to a variety of situations may be projected. Behaviorally more intricate than mice, rats have been the

A domesticated hooded rat, implanted with an electrode, aids science in the exploration of the mammalian brain.

central subjects for decades of psychological research, and their larger size permits easier handling for most applications where use of rodents is indicated. Because their physiology is similar to that of humans and other mammals, rats are in great favor with drug companies. These organizations, consuming more than eighteen million rats annually in the United States alone, sometimes profit from their errors as well as their successes in producing medicines; rats killed while being tested with new drugs are always examined by scientists interested in reducing rodent populations, and some of the brightest stars on the rat-poison horizon are drug-house booboos.

Domesticated rats have been selected over hundreds of generations in the manner of domesticated mice, but their behavior remains distinctly ratty. Because of their social inclinations, rats actually require a certain amount of handling, to which they look forward as to food and water. The response of domestic rats to humans is generally more complex than that of mice or other domesticated rodents, and individual rats may be taught to come when called by name. Outside, tame rats will follow on foot the human to whom they are most accustomed. These factors make domestic rats by far the most satisfactory of rodents as pets. In the United States the rodent pet industry makes its stockholders millions of dollars each year selling frivolous hamster- and gerbil-keeping outfits, and guinea pigs die by the millions from being mishandled and poorly fed by innocent little children. Syrian hamsters of the sort sold in pet stores are belligerent little beasts given to biting, and their relatives the Mongolian gerbils are similarly inclined. In addition these imported rodents pose an ecological danger in that they may escape and establish wild populations, potentially altering the environment as their relatives the rats have so often done in the past.

The sturdy domestic wanderratte is a good deal more intelligent and personable than these exotics and, unlike most other small animals, thrives on rough handling and table scraps. Also, contrary to popular belief, rats are meticulously clean animals, any filth with which they come in contact being the filth of human civilization. Properly cared for in the domestic situation, rats produce less odor than either hamsters or gerbils, and far less than the messy guinea pig, which passes large quantities of liquid urine. Some people cite the bare, scaled rat tail as an object of loathing, but this tail in itself is a curiosity and conversation piece, retained, as in mice, from the earliest mammals, a temperature-control device a hundred million years old. The domestic rat, in short, makes an elegant pet for persons who like tame rodents.

In many protein-short nations in Asia and Africa the rat is prized as a delicacy. Vietnam veterans will remember the Montagnard rat stew, which was actually very good if properly prepared, and in other poor countries the carcass of a rat brings a good price in market. In the Philippines, a group funded in part by the United States Agency for International Development is experimenting with marketing sausage made from the rats killed in rice paddies. Historically rats have always been eaten in times of siege and famine. During the siege of Malta in 1798 members of the French garrison paid exorbitant prices for dead rats, and in the Prussian siege of Paris in 1871 vast numbers of rats were roasted by the not-so-gay Parisians. Most eaters of rats prefer the meatier wander-ratte, which is said to taste rather like rabbit. Although a single rat is a meager meal for an adult human, it has been suggested that the key to rat eradication is to make the rat a delicacy of the table.

However, the elimination of rats will not come easily, if at all. Throughout their long association with us, we have been evolving devices to eliminate them, or at least to slow them down a little, and to absolutely no avail. We have tried trapping them. We use chokers, breakbacks, spear traps, barrel traps, mechanical repeating ratmash traps. We use snaptraps, steel traps, Havahart traps, Sherman collapsible and Mustang traps, and a million forgotten devices designed by individuals to fit their individual rat problems. We poison rats as we poison people at war. We drop tons of poisoned grain on them from airplanes, and we gas them with cyanide "A" dust, silently slaying them in the deeps of giant land-fills. We flood them out of their burrows with hoses and shoot them with rifles and chase them with dogs and cats and ferrets. We bury them with bulldozers and burn them in incinerators and dumps. We try locking them out with 26-gauge sheet steel, only to find that they swim through the sewers and come up in toilets. We seal the windows with heavy wire mesh, and the next night the rats come in through the air-conditioning ducts. We try keeping their food hidden, which means taking care of our own food, for what's ours is theirs. It also means taking care of our wastage. When New York City banned the use of incinerators in apartment buildings because of the air pollution to which they contributed, these same apartment buildings resorted to the use of basement trash compactors, in which, as it turned out, garbage was converted into rats as fast as it could be compacted. These were expensive apartment buildings harboring humans of alpha status, whose presence always demands efficient garbage disposal, and in many cases the managements of such buildings have been constrained by pride from reporting infestation by rats!

In the American ghettos, on the other hand, vast enclaves of humans of omega (bottom) status are sectioned off by their compatriots from many of the necessities of healthy and humane living. Here, of course, the waste problem is greater. Streets and lower levels of many buildings are roamed by predatory packs of adolescent males and drug-addicted peripheral humans, themselves victims of the social disintegration born of crowding. People living in the upper floors of these buildings toss their garbage out of the windows rather than descend to the unprotected ground floor, and the rats on the streets beneath feed on this garbage, increasing their numbers as the numbers of the poor increase. Blocks of empty, crumbling buildings become reservoirs of rats, brimming over with rodent prosperity, frothing with exuberant furry life in the midst of human decay.

The labors of the people of the United States of America, perhaps two hundred and thirty million strong, support an estimated population of one hundred and fifteen million rats, one rat to every two humans. Damage to property and foodstuffs by these rats, plus damage caused by rat-started fires, leaks, and so forth, not even counting the monetary costs of our puny efforts to reduce the rat population with "rat-control programs," costs the American people about ten dollars *per rat* per annum, more than a billion dollars in all. To gain perspective on what a billion dollars actually is, imagine that you are immortal and are alive at the presumed time of the birth of Christ, 25 December of the year 0. On this day you are given a billion dollars on one condition: that you spend precisely a *thousand dollars* of this money *per day,* every day of every year henceforth until the money is all gone. Not bad, huh? Well, you would still be spending that money today. As a matter of fact, you would still be spending that money in the year 2700! I wonder whether that could ever become boring, spending a thousand dollars a day. Anyway, instead of your spending it (or even better, *my* spending it), this money is literally poured down a rathole each year. It almost makes you want to cry, doesn't it?

America is a lucky land, a fluke, an aberrant stage in the history of the world resulting from the interaction of the technology of crowded Europe with the vast resources of a virgin continent. Raping the continent, the descendants of Europeans have built for themselves a living standard that will never again be shared by so many at one time on this planet. Americans of what we call "modest means" live in a world of material abundance that was unimaginable to the most decadent imperial Roman. In this comfortable place and time we and a few other favored groups in Europe and Japan share among ourselves the coveted alpha status, perhaps forgetting that it is the lot of the overwhelming majority of living humans to face the rat on his own level on a daily and nightly basis.

In Africa, Latin America, India, Pakistan, Laos, Cambodia, probably even China (though the Chinese won't admit it and it isn't fashionable to suspect them), in most of these places where so much human life is marginal, the rat reigns triumphant. There are religions imprisoning millions of human minds to the point where they actually resist attempts to control rats, believing that killing any animal for any reason is a sin. And in these same lands there are sudden plagues of rats engulfing acres of land in a single evening's orgiastic eating. A current estimate by the government of India puts the annual grain consumption of Indian rats at a volume sufficient to fill a freight train about 5000 kilometers long, or more than the breadth of the United States from New York to San Francisco. In Asia overall, an estimated forty-eight million tons of rice *alone* is eaten by rats annually, enough to feed two hundred and fifty million people, more than the population of the United States of America.

In the meantime, all the ingenious traps, all the virulent poisons, all the cunning predators domesticated by offended humanity have served to cause only momentary fluctuations in localized populations of rats. The world rat population rises in direct proportion to the world's human population, and neither species shows any sign of even faltering in its struggle toward whatever biological limit will slap it back to a healthy level. So we all enjoy living while we can, rats and humans. It's a good planet.

6 The Lesser Tenants

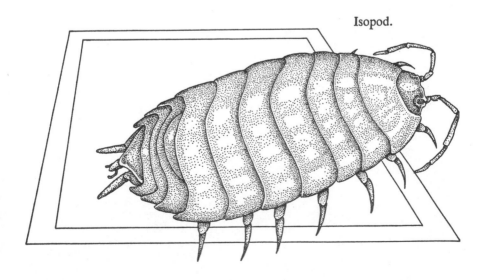

Isopod.

W e have been reading about the spectacular successes made by a few vertebrate species in invading the artificial system. Vertebrates, however, are but a drop in a zoological ocean composed largely of arthropods, "jointed-leggers," the most successful of all animal phyla and the dominant evolutionary pattern on this planet. Phylum Arthropoda has been around for a long time, and there are a lot more of them than there are of us. Their main formulas for success have been the evolution of their hard external skeletons and a fantastic rate of reproduction permitting rapid mutation in response to environmental changes.

The jointed skeleton for which arthropods are named enables them to move about on the land with ease. Because of this they are the only animal phylum other than vertebrates to have successfully invaded the terrestrial environment, in which gravity becomes a major problem in locomotion. The arthropod skeleton doubles as armor against the million assaults the environment offers to living matter. In order to increase in size, arthropods must occasionally molt the entire skeleton, replacing it with another more capacious one, and in this metabolically costly manner the arthropods grow.

Arthropods commonly lay hundreds or even thousands of eggs at a time, and if even two eggs in a laying survive, they can quickly reinstate a depleted population in times of environmental change. Thus

151

arthropods respond positively to almost any efforts on our part to destroy them, simply by mutating to meet our attacks. There is no individuality to speak of among the arthropods. Their brains are ganglia in which a complete environmental-interaction pattern is buried, much as a map may be buried in the memory of a cruise missile and recalled as the monster jets its inexorable way to its target. Nowhere else but among the arthropods is evolution so careless of the individual, so thoughtful of the type.

The history of the arthropods is intimately tied to that of our own phylum, the Chordata. Some seven hundred million years ago, at the beginning of the Paleozoic era, the oxygen level in the earth's atmosphere reached 1 percent or so, due to the activity of early photosynthesizers. The resultant increased availability of oxygen dissolved in the planetary ocean permitted a vast radiation of living forms and the establishment of most of the animal phyla alive today and many more that have since become extinct. On the scene at that momentous time were certain marine relatives of the modern earthworm, one of which was a worm called *Spriggina,* a humble beast who lived in the mud at the bottom of the sea. Little *Spriggina* had a number of appendages called parapodia that enabled it to move about more efficiently than some of its contemporaries, and it is likely that from such a form the first trilobites evolved.

The trilobites comprise one of the three great lines of arthropod evolution and probably the oldest. Trilobites were flattened, many-segmented armored creatures vaguely resembling the horseshoe crab *Limulus* of the Atlantic Coast, to which they probably gave rise. Trilobites first appeared during the lower Cambrian soon after the time of *Spriggina,* and quickly evolved into thousands of bizarre and intricate species. They were the dominant form of animal life on this planet for a hundred and seventy million years—compare our few thousand—a glorious evolutionary success in every sense of the word.

From the trilobites arose the next great line of arthropod evolution, the Mandibulata, including crustaceans and myriapods, such as centipedes and millipedes, and insects, the most successful form of terrestrial life. The Mandibulata possess one or two pairs of antennae, sensory appendages modified from the forelegs of some trilobitelike ancestor. They also have mandibles, as you have probably guessed, which are appendages modified to serve as paired jaws and which come in as many forms as there are species of Mandibulata. No one has any idea just how many species of these enormously successful animals there are, but the total is probably several million.

Very early in the evolution of the Mandibulata there was a separation of genetic lines leading to the founding of two great dynasties: class Crustacea and class Insecta. Class Crustacea is a group that early took to great motility in the water, diversifying quickly to master the smaller ecological niches in the Cambrian seas alongside their trilobite cousins. All the more familiar crustaceans—lobsters, crabs, crayfish, shrimp, barnacles, and their many, many relatives—live in aquatic environments, and most of them are marine. The members of one crustacean order, however, the Isopoda (same-leggers), have invaded the land with varying amounts of success. Most of the four thousand or so isopod species remain bound to a marine habitat, but some have been courageous enough to invade fresh water, a few have become parasites, and one suborder, the Oniscoidea, have come ashore as the pill bugs and sow bugs familiar to all of us. Sow bugs are the little segmented armored gray or brown beasts with seven pairs of legs of about equal length that one finds around plumbing and in dark places in houses. They are scavengers of the sorts of things their human landlords leave around. Being imperfectly adapted to land and to air-breathing, sow bugs must protect their gills by staying out of the sun and away from dryness. Consequently some species have come to inhabit humid, protected places among the works of humans, and by them have been transported all over the world. They are content to lead a peripheral existence in small moist places like our bathrooms and under our sinks, and rarely in their quiet lives do they bother us.

Distantly related to the isopods and possibly descended from them are the myriapods, a noncrustacean group of animals with what appear to us to be far too many legs. The order of Chilopods has contributed the house centipedes of the genus *Scutigera* to our towns and cities. These are extremely swift beings that, with their hairlike legs and antennae, sometimes resemble bits of dust blown by the wind. They hunt mainly by touch and smell, using their small eyes only to spot the movement of danger or the presence of light. That the reaction of human householders to these little hunters is almost invariably one of unparalled ferocity, usually culminating in death for the centipede, is a fact beyond explaining. The activity of house centipedes consists almost totally in an endless silent nocturnal patrol of the buildings in which they live in search of flies and other creatures inimical to pleasant living. House centipedes are automatic cleaning systems built into the ecology of the house, helping to keep the level of other arthropod inquilines down.

Two other classes of myriapods, the pauropods and symphylans, would not concern us directly except for the fact that it is from one of these, the Symphyla, that the insects are believed to have descended. Symphylans are small centipedelike animals having twenty-four legs and two long antennae. One genus, *Scutigerella,* the "garden centipede," has become an inquiline of controlled horticultural climate systems, better known as greenhouses. In these protected environments the little symphylans sometimes damage the roots and stems of plants.

Almost a million species in class Insecta have been described and at least as many more await description. Although the invention of flight is primarily responsible for the vast success of insects in the terrestrial environment, there are a few insect orders left over from the time three hundred million years ago when insects had no wings at all. One of these orders, the Thysanura (from the Greek meaning "tasseltails"), is a group of shy and retiring insects inhabiting moist earthy places and the protected environments constructed by human beings. Most familiar of these is probably the domestic silverfish, *Lepisma saccharina,* the ghostly gray teardrop-shaped insect one sees scurrying about in libraries. These animals are covered with delicate silver scales that come off at the slightest touch, making silverfish very slippery and hard to catch. Silverfish are lovers of starch and sugary substances, especially bookbinding glue, and are present wherever literate humans dwell. Another thysanuran species always associated with human dwellings is the firebrat, *Thermobia domestica,* a brown spirit of hearths and furnaces and other warm places. The hearth of the ancient human home was the place of cooking, of food-spilling and therefore of the scavenging firebrats. The descendants of these early inquilines inhabit oil furnaces, gas stoves, and the like, from which they emerge to scavenge leftovers. With their cousins the silverfish, firebrats share a cosmopolitan range.

After the rise of the Thysanura so long ago came the rise of flying insects, and with it the motility which was to win dominance for the class. We traveled some of the earlier history of flying insects in the chapter on pigeons so will only say here that it was their ability to fly and their rapid reproductive rate that made insects what they are today, occupants of every terrestrial econiche conceivable (and a good many inconceivable). There are twenty-three orders of insects descended from those that first took to the air, comprising more than seven hundred thousand described species and at least as many more as yet unknown. Members of several of these orders have made a specialty of living in human food-distribution systems, and it would be impossible to take more than the very briefest look at the contributions our culture makes to the well-being of class Insecta.

Starting at the bottom of the family tree of flying insects, we find an order known as the Orthoptera, "straight-wings." These are probably close to the origins of flight in insects, and they are mightily successful, having retained through the aeons a large cut of the world's ecological pie. Most orthopterans, including especially the grasshoppers and crickets, are herbivores, but a few aberrant forms such as mantids may be voracious carnivores. The order also embraces the famous cockroaches of family Blattidae. (Almost all cockroach inquilines can fly; they generally do so when very warm or when feeling sexy and looking for a partner. If they don't fly at your house, that is because you haven't asked them politely. Drop one out a window on a warm day sometime.)

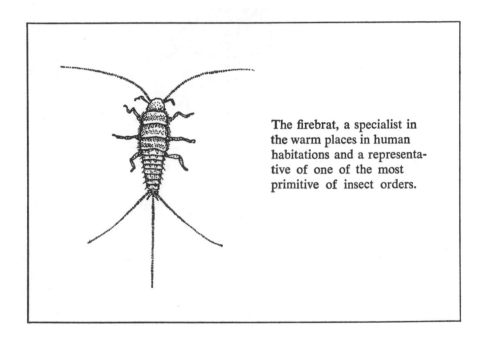

The firebrat, a specialist in the warm places in human habitations and a representative of one of the most primitive of insect orders.

There are several species of cockroaches living among humans, and the inhabitants of large cities enjoy telling one another gory cockroach stories. Dating from the late Carboniferous era, roaches eat anything at all, and because it is precisely this substance that is most frequently spilled in human habitations, these generalized insects do very well there. Cockroaches come equipped with a stinking defensive chemical that causes kittens and puppies eating them to throw them right up and abandon the habit. This repellent odor, familiar to city dwellers around the world, also serves to attract other roaches, so that entire colonies may live behind one stove. Although there are many species of cockroaches around the warmer parts of the world, only five species have successfully taken the inquiline route with humanity.

The American cockroach, *Periplaneta americana,* probably a native of Africa, has traveled across the milder parts of the globe in conjunction with human trade. In northerly climates, such as New York, where the winter is noticeable, American cockroaches are confined to buildings and subways and other places where people are messy and inconsiderate to

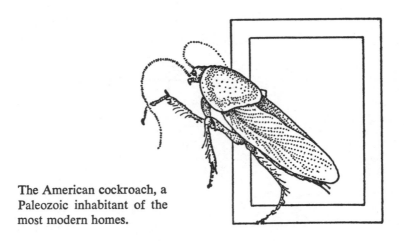

The American cockroach, a Paleozoic inhabitant of the most modern homes.

one another. In the same genus, *Periplaneta,* is the Australian cockroach, *P. australasiae,* which is similarly distributed all around the world by human activity.

The Oriental cockroach, *Blatta orientalis,* is another worldwide species. The male of this species has very short wings and the female is entirely flightless, with vestigial wing buds only. These roaches tend to confine their activity to areas where dirt is easily available, and thus rarely go higher than the first floors of buildings. The tropical cockroach, *Supella supellertilium,* and the German roach, *Blatella germanica,* like the roaches discussed above, practice egg protection by carrying their eggs about in leathery capsules called ootheca. The eggs are carefully stowed away in some safe place before hatching, so that the young roaches are more likely to survive than are the young of insects whose eggs are unprotected and subject to predation. The German roach concentrates its activity around plumbing and is the "water bug" of the apartment-dweller's lexicon.

Roaches like moist, warm areas, such as overheated apartments, basements, and sewers. Where the climate is dry there may be fewer roaches, but any warm building where food is allowed to stray from its intended path will support a population. In the domestic situation roaches consume foods, fabric, and the starchy contents of bookbindings. In addition they carry any filth with which they come in contact and thus spread diseases, such as dysentery, by contaminating foodstuffs.

The rapid reproductive and mutation rate of cockroaches is responsible for their alarming ability to adapt to poisoning—to such a degree that their bodies may actually store life-destroying substances spread in their paths by their human landlords. In many cases this accumulation of poisons is enough to kill animals preying on roaches, as often happens to pet birds and other household fauna. Roaches are sturdy animals, occasionally living several years (most insects live less than a year). Because of this sturdiness roaches are often used in experiments dealing with insect physiology.

Distantly related to the roaches in the same order is the house cricket, *Acheta domesticus*. These modest dark insects of the night live outdoors, in artificial situations like gardens and dumps, when it is warm, tending in winter to return to houses for warmth. They are nearly omnivorous, eating woolen clothing, some garden plants, dried meat, and anything else that happens to be around. These inquilines are famed for their pleasant nocturnal chirping, which nearly cancels out the irritation of having the things running about underfoot in the dark. The music of the house cricket has earned it the affection of humans worldwide. European Celts were among the earliest peoples to believe that a cricket on the hearth is good luck; Oriental peoples have long kept crickets in elaborate bamboo or wooden cages, feeding them lettuce and other vegetables. If several cages are so maintained, the inmates will keep up a pleasant chorus through any warm night.

Clambering a bit farther up the insect evolutionary ladder we come to the order Psocoptera, the "book louse-wings," another fairly primitive winged group dating from the Paleozoic era. These are minute insects which would go unnoticed except for *Lepinotus inquilinus* and its relatives the book lice. Like thysanurans, book lice frequent libraries and other places where large quantities of dry materials may be found. Book lice make a variety of tiny ticking and groaning noises with precise and even spacing between them. For centuries these ghostly noises have frightened superstitious people, and one species, *Trogium pulsatorium,* is called the deathwatch, although its noise is actually a mating call. Members of the family Psyllipsocidae prefer acid, damp places such as wine cellars, which is possibly what makes them so psylli in the first place.

Thus ungracefully transcending the Psocoptera, we arrive at the Lepidoptera, the "scaled-winged ones," the large, advanced order containing butterflies and moths. These insects differ from those we have so far examined in that they undergo a complete metamorphosis from a larval form called a caterpillar into a winged adult, occupying two completely different ecological niches in one lifetime. It is probably the evolution of this dual life that enabled the higher insects (those with complete metamorphosis) to assume the commanding place they occupy in the ecology of the world. Perhaps the best-known lepidopteran inquiline is the clothes moth, *Tineola biselliella,* an inhabitant of stored animal-based textiles, such as expensive wool sweaters. It should here be noted that the clothes moth is a *very small* yellowish moth (less than a centimeter long), and that the large handsome moths attracted to lights do *not* eat clothes. Meal moths of the genus Pyralis and grain moths of the genera Sitotroga and Angoumois are found wherever grain and other vegetable matter are stored, and these have traveled to all parts of the world in conjunction with human trade.

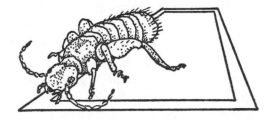

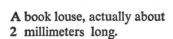
A book louse, actually about 2 millimeters long.

The largest of all insect orders, the most diverse, and the most expert in exploiting the diverse resources of the planet is the order Coleoptera, the "sheath-wings," the tough and resilient beetles. There are beetles everywhere. There are beetles so small that they are nearly invisible to the naked eye, and there are beetles many centimeters long, outweighing mice and small birds in their armored magnificence. The Coleoptera owe their evolutionary achievement to the design of their fore wings. Like most flying insects, beetles possess four wings arranged in two pairs, one fore and one aft. It is only the hind wings of beetles that do the flying, the fore wings having been modified to form leathery protective sheaths beneath which the delicate flying pair may be folded out of the way when not in use. Thus a beetle may rummage about in the most improbably small places without damage to its aerial travel system, and in this way the beetles have successfully invaded most of the seemingly infinite variety of cryptic microhabitats available to land animals. There are some five hundred thousand described species of beetles, depending on whose entomology you prefer, and it is no great surprise that the majority of our herbivorous inquilines are beetles. Although they annoy and injure us with their depredations, the hundreds of species of beetles who are our tenants are also representatives of life at its ebullient best. Indeed, the gemlike beauty and diversity of the beetles within the artificial ecosystem are tributes to the complexity of our civilization.

Beetles of the family Dermestidae are familiar to anyone who has ever dried meat for jerky or who has tried to maintain an insect collection without protecting it with fumigants. Dermestids are scavengers, feeding on dried organic matter such as untanned leather, museum specimens, rugs, stored grains, furs, and the like. Vertebrate zoologists, including the author, sometimes maintain colonies of dermestids, with which dried vertebrate skeletons may be cleaned for study. In this regard dermestids are very clean and efficient, but the limited scholarly use of the beetles hardly offsets the damage they do to fine Middle Eastern carpets alone. Many a collection of rare insects or bird skins has also been ruined by dermestid activity. Dermestid larvae do most of the species' work. They are conical M.C. Escher productions armed with a symmetrical array of barbed spines to deter predators. These spines are hair-thin and very brittle, and to insect-sized hunters act as quills with which, porcupinelike, the inoffensive larva is defended. When a colony of larvae is disturbed by a larger animal, such as a vertebrate zoologist, the spines break off by the thousands, filling the air and (painfully) the upper respiratory tract of whatever dummy presumed to bother dermestids in the first place.

After molting several times, dermestid larvae pupate, going through a marvelous period of quiescent transition from a blunt-ended spiny wormlike eating machine to an armored flying gene-dispersal machine. This bullet-shaped adult beetle buzzes through the air, sometimes visiting flowers on the way but always searching for a likely food-rich place such as an animal carcass or a ham in which to mate and lay its seventy or so eggs. The eggs hatch into more larvae, and the process is repeated like some organic fireworks display, the larvae growing, changing, soaring through the air as adults, hitting a ham, and whacko! seventy more larvae spread across the ham like embers falling in the night, to grow and mature and fly again. The best known dermestid is probably the larder beetle, *Dermestes lardarius,* which has traveled across the entire planet in conjunction with dried foods carried on shipboard.

Sharing the ranges of humans and dermestids is the ham beetle, *Necrobia rufipes,* of the family Cleridae. These brilliantly metallic blue or green beetles, about 5 millimeters long, prey on the larvae of dermestids and other insects that invade stored meats, grain, and other dry goods. Because their larvae bore through meats and cheeses, ham beetles are said to be pests; however, no ham beetle worth its bacon will touch any food not already infested with other inquilines, and therefore the presence of ham beetles can be said to be a symptom of a deeper problem in food storage.

The Ostomidae, or "grain-gnawing beetles," are represented in our larders by the granary beetle, *Tenebroides mauritanicus.* About a centimeter long, the adults of this species are black or brown and deeply sculpted with linear grooves and bosses. Their young infest stored vegetable matter and, like the adults, can bore through wooden walls to reach food. *T. mauritanicus* shares the range of those *H. sapiens* who eat grain.

The sawtoothed grain beetle, *Oryzaephilus surinamensis,* is also a lover of tobacco, candy, sugar, grains, dried meats, dried fruits, and almost any other dry organic matter. These minute insects are believed to have been introduced to world commerce by the Dutch colonists in South America, to which the beetles are native. Other eaters of stored foodstuffs come from the great family Tenebrionidae, the "darkling beetles," of which there are some two thousand species in the United States alone. Familiar to little kids who like hot cereal is the confused flour beetle, *Tribolium confusum,* named for its lunatic scurrying about when dumped out of the morning oatmeal. These common red-brown 3-millimeter beetles are found in stored grains throughout the world and are often used in population-genetics experiments because their breeding cycle is so short. Flour beetles made the news recently when they extended their range to the households of Houlton, Maine. In May of 1977, legions of the tiny insects emerged from a grain elevator to conquer Houlton's pantries, so infuriating the sturdy Yankee citizens of that town that echoes of the fray reached even *The Wall Street Journal.* One entomologist, ignorant of the ecology of inquilinism, suggested that the beetles would be killed by Houlton's severe winter—ignoring, of course, the fact that the beetles live with Houlton's citizens because these people are wise enough to keep their houses *warm* during the cold months. Besides, even one surviving fertile pair of flour beetles, unchecked, might found a dynasty of several billion descendants during a year's orgiastic reproduction. Chalk up one more for the flour beetle.

Another tenebrionid, the lesser mealworm, *Alphitobius diaperinus,* eats not only stored grains and cereals, but the carcasses of dead domestic animals and broken poultry eggs. These animals transmit poultry diseases when they take up residence around poultry yards, their favorite habitat. The plain old mealworm, *Tenebrio molitor,* is familiar to anyone who has ever kept exotic birds, tropical fish, or small reptiles and amphibians. Raised by the pet industry as food for insectivorous pets, the larvae of these dark 1.5-centimeter-long beetles infest stored grains of all sorts and defend themselves with a chemical stink. They are global in distribution.

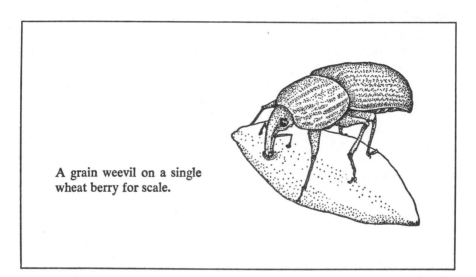

A grain weevil on a single wheat berry for scale.

The false powder-post beetles of the family Bostrichidae contribute a well-known inquiline of grain stores, the lesser grain borer, *Rhyzopertha dominica,* which originated in some warm place long ago and in the old familiar fashion took to us with enthusiasm. Lesser grain borers are among the most damaging pests of stored foods and are of course familiar worldwide. A host of spider beetles of the family Ptinidae occupy niches overlapping that of the lesser grain borer. Spider beetles are minute, humpbacked animals rather resembling their namesakes and occurring in enormous numbers in warehouses, homes, granaries, and anywhere else we keep edibles. Spider beetles and their larvae feed on dried meats, spices, dead insects, grains, textiles, books, sugar, leather, cereals, and even such poisonous substances as tobacco and opium.

The deathwatch and drugstore beetles of the family Anobiidae have moved into some unique niches in the human ecosystem. Deathwatch beetles, named for a tapping habit similar to that of the psocids, are specialized in the reduction of seasoned timber in buildings and furniture. They have been transported across the world's temperate zones where wood is commonly used in building. Drugstore and cigarette beetles tend to prefer cities. Remains of both species were found in the tomb of Tutankhamen, having been inquilines of the bounty of Pharaoh three thousand years ago. The drugstore beetle, *Stegobium paniceum,* eats drugs, which it appears to like very much. When unable to reach the proper fix, however, these beetles cheerfully take to granaries and other food storehouses. Their cousin the cigarette beetle, *Lasioderma serricorne,* is an elegant, tobacco-colored lover of dried products of the poisonous plants of genus *Nicotiana,* prospering generation after generation in stores of the leaves. In Tutankhamen's tomb, where there was no tobacco, the cigarette beetles made do with spices and perfumes.

The largest family of insects, which includes perhaps fifty thousand species, is the Curculionidae, the "snout beetles" commonly called weevils. These animals triumphed with the invention of a long snout bearing at its tip the gnawing mandibles, enabling them to bore deep holes and to conceal their eggs in the centers of peas and other unlikely places. The larvae thus grow in a little container of food, protected from the trials and tribulations of a free-roaming existence, and have consequently degenerated more than is common among beetle larvae to become simple grubs without eyes or legs.

Probably best known of the inquiline weevils is the granary weevil, *Sitophilus granarius,* about 3 millimeters in length, a wingless form that bores into grain, where the eggs are laid. Each larva grows within a single grain of wheat, oats, or other seed, requiring about a month to mature to the adult stage and begin the process again. A close relative, the rice weevil, *S. oryzae,* retains wings even though it leads a similarly easy life in stored rice. Together these cousins convert vast quantities of grain into beetles and are justly famed and feared among the commodity brokers of the world. They live in any part of the globe where grain is kept by humans.

Other things besides insects, rats, and mice eat our stored products. Many fungi have taken up a comfortable existence in human possessions, and an assemblage of tiny beetles has adopted a secondary consumer position wherever these fungi occur. Collectively called fungus beetles, these animals hail from three small families which have been distributed throughout the world in our ships and other conveyances. They compound the fungus problems of stored goods by serving as vectors for the spores of the fungi they eat, carrying these spores from place to place in their movement.

Two remaining higher orders of insects, while enormously successful independent of human beings, have a surprisingly poor representation among the inquilines. The Diptera, the "two-winged flies," are represented in our households mainly by the family Muscidae, including the various houseflies, latrine flies, stable, face, and dump flies. These species, all similar enough to one another to be covered in one description, have inherited the cosmopolitan distribution that is the reward of successful inquilinism with humanity. The house fly, *Musca domesticus,* probably originated somewhere in the Eastern Hemisphere when humans first became sedentary and began accumulating garbage of the nastier sort. It is significant that the larval stage of the housefly's life *must* be spent in wet, putrefying masses of organic matter. Thus the population of house flies in any area is in direct proportion to the availability of exposed wet, putrid organic matter, and consequently the social conditions and level of ecological enlightenment of a people or political system may in part be evaluated by the population of houseflies present.

Houseflies leave two varieties of flyspecks, both of which are familiar to humans all over the world. The common yellow blob found on the pages of open books is regurgitated food—fly vomit—while the dark flecks are fly crap. With these flyspecks and their feet, houseflies transmit the eggs of tapeworms, pinworms, and hookworms to their human landlords. Flyspecks may also contain the seeds of typhoid fever, cholera, infectious hepatitis, and a dozen varieties of Montezuma's Revenge, San Antonio Fever, Greasy Spoon, and other familiar disorders of the human intestinal tract. Houseflies may also be responsible for the present distribution of human populations in that they are believed to have been the greatest menace to human health of any insect within historical times.

Houseflies lay seventy-five to a hundred eggs in any appropriately moist and nutritious yuck, such as human excrement, manure, or good rich garbage. The eggs hatch within a day to produce larvae that are little more than sacs of fat and digestive equipment. These sacs propel themselves through their disgusting food by means of two hooks where the head would have been if these were free-living animals rather than mere swimmers through putrescence. A close relative of the housefly, the little housefly *Fannia canicularis,* replaces the regular brand in cold northern climates. With larvae of their congeneric the latrine fly, *Fannia scalaris,* these larvae may infest the ears and intestines of living human beings, causing the horrible condition known as myiasis. Human innards are also sometimes subject to invasion by larvae of the false stable fly, *Muscina stabulans,* which lays its eggs in dairy products and meats.

Considered from an anthropocentric point of view, the econiches of muscid flies almost transcend the limits of polite conversation, but as members of the great order of two-winged flies these animals are worthy of at least a moment's notice. Whereas most other insects have four wings arranged in two pairs, the Diptera have only fore wings for flying. The hind wings have been reduced to a pair of halteres, which are club-shaped organs that vibrate rapidly up and down as the fly flies. Because the halteres are relatively dense in their knob-shaped tips, they resist movement out of their plane of orientation much as a spinning gyroscope does, providing the aerial orientation system of the fly with a superb sensor of directional change. As anyone who has ever swatted flies knows, the little monsters are ungodly fast and free in flight, and it is this gyroscopic sensor that is responsible for much of their success.

The last insect order to invade our artificial system was the Hymenoptera, the "membrane-wings," which include the wasps, bees, ants, and many less familiar forms. Most hymenopterans are hunters and nectar-feeders that avoid the denser haunts of humans, but one species of ant has been distributed worldwide in association with human commerce. This is the pharaoh ant, *Monomorium pharaonis,* the tiny (2-millimeter) yellowish creature that invades our kitchens and larders for almost any exposed organic matter. Called "pissants" by people in the American South, pharaoh ants are attracted to sweets, including particularly the sugar in urine, and to grease and meats. Pharaoh ants are originally from Africa, but by now you know how these things go.

Most ant colonies reproduce in a nuptial flight, during which the winged sexual forms (queens and males) mate in the air, and after which the males die and the fertilized females establish new colonies with themselves as queens. Pharaoh ants represent a significant departure from this mode, a necessary change in adopting the houses of humans as their preferred environment. Rather than scattering their seed across the landscape in nuptial flights, the colonies of pharaoh ants branch off from parent colonies as little groups of fifty or so workers carrying larvae, led by one or two of the wingless queens characteristic of the species. Thus many groups may spread through the walls of a building as one colony buds over a period of time.

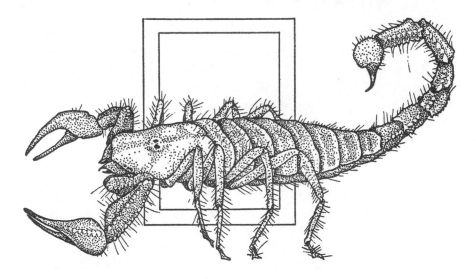

A house scorpion, member of a group that has remained essentially unchanged for four hundred million years.

Active colonies of these ants range in size from as few as fifty to over a thousand workers, and larger colonies can contain up to a hundred queens. Colonies located in the same building often share the trails by which ants locate food and water, and can thus be said to compose a supercolony living off the messes in that building. When a colony strains at the limits of its resources, a nestwide restlessness results, and larvae are transported from place to place in a feverish, seemingly random fashion. If the stress is not alleviated, budding takes place until a stable situation is reached. Interestingly, budding groups of pharaoh ants are able to raise fertile queens and males from the larvae they carry even if none accompany them on their trek. This further ensures the survival of their kind in the unpredictable human environment, where the migrating wingless males and queens might be subject to attack by their landlords. In abandoning nuptial flights, pharaoh ants have lost the ability to make rapid dispersal movements across a landmass as their less specialized relatives do, but by adopting the budding technique they have completely saturated the ecological niches available to ants in the artificial system.

These are a very few of the arthropods that make use of the artificial system. It is easy to understand that any human house containing little gnawers of food and creepers along baseboards might also support a collection of tiny predators designed to feed off this extensive miniature fauna. Class Arachnida, the mighty group containing spiders, scorpions, and other less familiar forms, has contributed a startling assortment of predators perfectly designed to keep some of the insect populations under control in our houses. Although we rarely see our household arachnids, they are always there, doing their silent and efficient best to reduce the numbers of our smaller tenants.

The arachnids represent the third great arthropod line of evolution the Chelicerata. Chelicerates usually possess six pairs of appendages, the first of which are often modified to form jawlike mouth-parts called chelicerae. The earliest chelicerates seem to have been descended from trilobites and were horseshoe-crab-shaped forms, from which are descended our modern Atlantic horseshoe crabs.

From these early forms descended the first Eurypterids, the "broad-wings," primitive arthropods commonly called giant water scorpions. These frightening animals achieved dominance in the oceans of the past, often reaching lengths of more than 3 meters and possibly weighing several hundred kilograms. Eurypterids were characteristically elongated, active animals with the abdominal portion divided into twelve articulated segments reminiscent of those of their ancestors, the trilobites. The foremost segment, termed the cephalothorax or "head-chest," came equipped with a large pair of chelicerae rather like scorpion "claws." The tail or telson was probably fitted with a poisonous sting, with which the eurypterids deactivated their prey, for these were the fiercest predators of the primal seas. Most were equipped with two large forward-directed compound eyes and two smaller eyes, ocelli, on top of the cephalothorax. The eurypterids apparently swam upside-down, in the manner of some modern aquatic insects, and could move rapidly after prey. It is likely that the early vertebrates from which we are ultimately descended found life perilous with the eurypterids about, and the fossil record suggests that the lucky evolution of predaceous armored vertebrate forms was the only factor capable of ridding the oceans of eurypterids. The eurypterids flourished through the Silurian and Devonian periods from four hundred and thirty million to three hundred and forty million years ago, finally becoming extinct in conjunction with the rise of fish. And we don't miss them a bit.

From the eurypterids or a similar form the arachnids produced a line to exploit a biological revolution which occurred some four hundred million years ago, when the oxygen in the earth's atmosphere is believed to have risen to 10 percent for the first time and an invasion of the land by animals resulted. The first arthropods to have evolved the efficient "book lungs" widespread in the class were able to spend some time along the seashore, and from these the remainder of the mighty class Arachnida is descended. Scorpions, the oldest known arachnids, date from the Silurian period four hundred million years ago, and it is probably from these bizarre and ancient forms that the entire class of spiders, harvestmen, pseudoscorpions, ticks, mites, and other oddities evolved and triumphed.

It is hardly surprising that creatures so good at the game of life as the scorpions, so ancient and wise and perfect, should find a way to exploit the habitations of humans. In fact, they often do this in numbers great enough to constitute a threat to their landlords. One of the scorpion's evolutionary aces in the hole is the possession of the famous stinger at the end of its thin, highly articulated abdomen or "tail." This stinger is equipped with two glands producing a toxin poisonous to the nervous systems of most animals. The pedipalps, or second appendages, of scorpions are modified into grasping claws similar to those of a tiny lobster, and it is with these that prey is seized. The long tail bearing the sting is then brought over the creature's head, such as it is, and driven into the prey, immobilizing it. With the sting some scorpions can damage animals much larger than themselves; those of the genus Centruroides of the southwestern United States have even been known to kill human children. However, by and large, scorpions are inoffensive beasts that may charm one with their ancient and noble lineage.

In the human context scorpions remain predators, as they have been for hundreds of millions of years. Feeding on any insect inquilines into which they can sink their pedipalps, our household scorpions should perhaps be welcome; it is, after all, only when they are attacked or stepped on or otherwise threatened that scorpions will employ the dreaded sting against vertebrates like ourselves. Millions of people in nations around the world live in houses well stocked with scorpions without even seeing them, let alone being stung. Viewed close up, the many species of household scorpions are beautiful in their glistening armor. The surface of this armor is embossed with ridges and rows of plates and spines, giving their possessors much of the visual appeal of certain elaborate seashells and other skeletal formations of living matter. The movements of the scorpion are impressive in themselves, for they give us a glimpse of the first mode of locomotion that seems to have made it in the terrestrial environment. Scorpions are highly active, as befits their predatory nature, and they move with a certain grace, as if flowing across the floor, with pedipalps held at the ready like tiny steel traps. Much of a scorpion's existence is oriented around tactile stimuli, for scorpions are nocturnal and poorly equipped visually. The characteristic, raised pedipalps close instantly and automatically when the hunting scorpion blunders into some prey, and the stinging reflex is equally automatic.

Unlike so many other arthropod inquilines, scorpions help to keep a lid on the activities of our competitors while adding a picturesque touch themselves to the household ecology. They offer the human observer a bit of the ancient and terrible drama of Silurian life more than four hundred million years ago to spice the secure boredom of apartment life. If you are lucky enough to see one of the little ogres slipping along your baseboard, give him a moment of your time, watch him go about his age-old business of pouncing on his cousins within your walls. He is a good man, the scorpion, old and wise. Give him his due—don't squash him.

Closely related to the old scorpion, and probably descended from

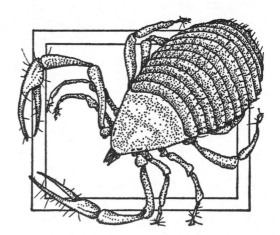

The house pseudoscorpion, or "book scorpion," inhabitant of the Gutenberg galaxy.

him, are several lesser orders of arachnids whose appearance is more or less scorpionlike even though they include strictly stingless and harmless (to humans) little predators. Among these lesser orders are the tailed and tailless whip scorpions, which specialize in dark places containing insects, such as the undersides of refrigerators and the backs of stoves and other appliances. Most tailless whip scorpions, Amblypygi, named for their long thin tactile forelegs, prefer to live in desert or semidesert environments where there are plenty of hiding places for use during the daylight hours. At night, those that have taken up residence in houses come out and run along the bases of walls, where they are able to pick off a few of the many other species of arthropods sharing this habitat.

The tailed whip scorpions, Uropygi, possess pedipalps modified to grasp prey; these are equipped with piercing spines. At the end of the twelve-segmented abdomen is a long thin tail at whose base is a pair of glands producing a strong defensive odor. Reminiscent of formic or acetic acid, this odor has earned these creatures the nickname "vinegaroon" wherever they are common. Like true scorpions, whip scorpions are fast-moving and graceful but rarely seen predators that are an asset to any household. In many cases individuals representative of the tailed and tail-less whip scorpion groups are strikingly beautiful little animals, well worth some close scrutiny.

The arachnid order Pseudoscorpionida, the (you guessed it) pseudo-scorpions, includes a genus that makes a specialty of hunting the insects that are inquilines of book collections. Unlike true scorpions, pseudo-scorpions lack a long tail with a sting, being equipped instead with venom glands in their pinching pedipalps (which are entirely harmless to humans). Because of their small size (less than 5 millimeters in length), pseudoscorpions are rarely seen unless they somehow become trapped in bathtubs or sinks, where they seek moisture. The book scorpion or house pseudoscorpion, *Chelifer cancroides,* one of the largest of the order at some 4 millimeters, has been transported by humans from some unknown point of origin to the entire surface of the globe, or at least to every place where books are kept. This voracious little predator feeds on psocid and thysanuran insects in libraries and may also enter closets and capture both larvae and adults of clothes moths. In addition, *Chelifer* sometimes attacks bedbugs, which are said to be a favorite prey, as well as carpet beetles. Viewed through a hand lens or miscroscope, the pseudoscorpions can be seen to be beautifully equipped with highly or-namental armor, surpassing the best produced by the armorers of medi-eval Europe. In the community of smaller inquilines inhabiting our cities and towns, *Chelifer* and its relatives must be fearsome predators indeed; we know they are assets to the literary works of humanity.

Perhaps more familiar to householders than the scorpions are the members of the order Phalangida, the harvestmen or daddy longlegs. More than three thousand species of the order have been cataloged, in-cluding a number which seem to prefer the houses of humans, especially in regions where the winters are hard and the asphalt thick. Unlike most arachnids, these little animals may eat both insects and decaying vegetable matter, being especially fond of aphids and other small beasts that plague horticulturists around the world. Although they are not immediately visible on casual inspection of harvestmen, the chelicerae are powerful and equipped in many cases with pinchers with which the prey is crushed. The delicate appearance of harvestmen may seem out of character with their usually predatory habits; their fragile, threadlike legs seem too delicate for any catch-as-catch-can. For eating the sedentary, soft-bodied insects on which they specialize, however, the build of harvestmen is perfect. In almost any cellar or basement, or in dark places beneath the larger appliances, harvestmen await the night and the safety of darkness, in which they may run about unnoticed by stronger animals. As anyone who has touched a harvestman knows, their long legs are designed to break along special points of weakness if held for an instant. This breaking is a process called autotomy, which is common to animals of many phyla. "He who pulls and breaks away lives to hunt another day," as the saying goes. Whereas most arachnids are designed with a narrowing of the body between the cephalothorax and the abdomen, harvestmen seem to have ovoid or nearly spherical little bodies with almost no visible division between the two sections. Hung from the arches of the long legs, these bodies give harvestmen a comical appearance familiar to children around the world. Here is another inquiline that is a blessing to the human community and an object of beauty in its own right.

The largest order of arachnids is the Acarina, the mites, so diverse that the twenty-five thousand or so species that have been described are estimated to be only a small fraction of those with which our planet is blessed (or cursed, depending on the mite concerned). Many mites are parasitic—some inhabit specialized niches such as the air sacs of pigeons, while other acarine parasites live in such restricted places as the eyelids of mammals, the nostrils of birds, the armpits of bats, or the lungs of monkeys. Many more mites are predators, feeding on other small animals with whom they share their habitats. Relatively few mites are inquilines, and those that do choose to share our homes with us are ordinarily too small (less than a millimeter long) to be seen unless they are carefully searched out. Perhaps most familiar of the inquiline mites are the cheese mites of the suborder Sarcoptiformes, which inhabit stored goods and sometimes attack the skin of humans, causing a rash called "grocer's itch." It is probable that thousands upon thousands of mites are inquilines of humans in various parts of the world, but the study of this vast order is still in its infancy. Because of the many diseases they may carry and the frequency with which they attack humans and domestic animals, mites are often much feared and hated. However, in the ultimate balance, the

Acarina may be considered beneficial to humans, for the predaceous and parasitic species live in many cases on competitors of ours.

The most familiar order of arachnids, and one of the largest, is the Araneae, the spiders, of which thousands of species have at one time or another invaded the human ecosystem. Spiders are probably descended from a scorpionlike ancestor and first occur in the fossil record from Devonian times three hundred and forty-five million years ago. The word "spiders" is derived from Danish *spinder,* "spinner," and of course refers to the silk-spinning adaptation that is primarily responsible for the immense success of the order. Spiders number some fifty thousand species, and probably twice as many more are as yet undescribed. Spiders come in a large range of sizes, from as small as 0.3 millimeter to nearly 10 centimeters in length. All spiders are predators, the most familiar forms building silk snares with which they trap their arthropod prey.

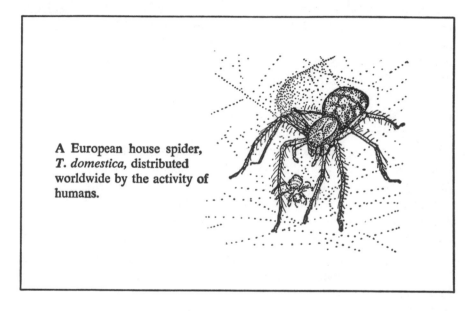

A European house spider, *T. domestica,* distributed worldwide by the activity of humans.

A number of species of spiders are found mainly in the buildings of humans, where they share with their arachnid cousins a diet of other small inquilines. Perhaps the most familiar spiders in human houses are the house spiders of the genera *Achaearanea* and *Theridion,* whose irregular webs are the "cobwebs" that appear in almost any indoor nook or cranny. These delicate animals are so completely adapted to hanging around upside down in their webs that they are inefficient at walking on flat surfaces and are rarely seen moving about. Because of their dependence on stable support for the all-important web, house spiders early took up residence in the habitations of humans, where wind is infrequent, temperature steady, and housecleaning indifferent. Female house spiders are often seen tending their egg sacs, ovoid papery balls of a beige color stored in corners and other out-of-the-way places. The males, whose legs are orange, and females, whose legs are yellow, are often found in the same web, where they may mate repeatedly, although such associations are due more to chance than to actual pair-bonding.

In Europe and Asia originated various species of spiders of the genus *Tegenaria,* the European house spiders, whose ways are quite different from those of the house spiders described above. European house spiders are members of the family Agelenidae, the "funnel-web weavers," whose snare is a horizontal sheet liberally sprung with message-wires that penetrate a silk funnel in which the spider itself lives. When prey strikes the surface of the densely woven sheet, the silk lines to the funnel alert the proprietor, who emerges and seizes the prey and then immediately returns to the protected funnel to eat in privacy. The silk webs of Agelenidae are often visible in great profusion on fields and lawns in the morning dew, one of the most familiar and yet most beautiful offerings of the kindly earth to the human eye.

The European house spiders also build such webs in dark, moist places, where our smaller inquilines are most likely to be moving about. A few species inhabit North America and are familiar to almost anyone who cleans out a basement or an attic. The female of genus *Tegenaria* is a notable mother among the arthropods, tending her young with great care, signaling them for food with special movements of the web. In a similar manner she signals them to cover when danger approaches, and she is never uncouth enough to mistake the movements of one of her spiderlets for prey. The European house spiders are active runners with strong jaws and fairly sharp eyes. Many of these spiders are furred like tiny cats, often as beautifully marked in brown and gray and tabby. Living in shining silken funnels as they do, they add a touch of elegance in miniature to rooms that are all too often drab and dreary—and, in addition, they eat cockroaches. Beauty and utility—an unbeatable combination.

Sac spiders of the genus *Chiracanthium,* which originally lived around the Mediterranean, have followed the ancient inquiline route with Europeans to most of the world's cities and towns. These are hunting spiders that use no snares, preferring to run their prey down and tackle it by force. During the day sac spiders weave their namesake sacs, silken tubes open at both ends, in which they sleep and the eggs are sometimes guarded. Occasionally one of these spiders will bite a human, raising quite a welt, but this is a rare occurrence. Few spiders can be induced to bite, and of those that will bite at all, only a tiny proportion can do any damage. The "spider bites" we receive while asleep in the summer actually result from the ministrations of certain nocturnal flies, which are far more dangerous than spiders because of diseases they may carry.

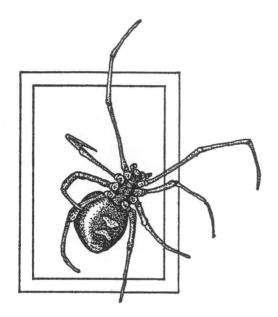

The black widow, jewellike in glossy black, a specialist in houseflies. In this specimen the famous hourglass marking on the abdomen is divided.

However, there are spiders that *can* do us harm, and these are also common inquilines. Perhaps the best known is the black widow spider, *Lactrodectus mactans,* which lives near and in human habitations around the world as far north as Canada and the Soviet Union and as far south as the southern tip of Africa. Black widows inhabit houses and other buildings, dumps, bridges, and trash piles, where they may be responsible for bringing down a large number of houseflies. Black widows are also responsible for most of the very few cases of humans envenomated by spiders. It is inevitable that at certain times the paths of human and inquiline cross, and the female black widow is a touchy subject if shouldered about, mashed, or otherwise inconvenienced by her blundering landlord. Interestingly, one of the more common locations of black widow attacks on humans is in the nether portions, precisely those parts fitting over the little hole in the privy. The high concentration of house flies ordinarily

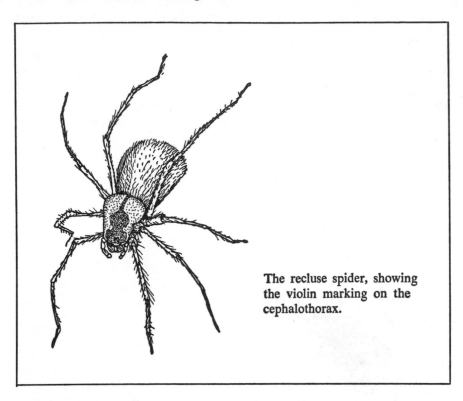

The recluse spider, showing the violin marking on the cephalothorax.

present in this lucrative microhabitat make it a natural for widows, which, after all, love us only for our flies, and the disrupting presence of people in the privy is sometimes resented. The venom of the widow attacks the nervous system, producing intense and agonizing contractions of the abdominal muscles. The victim salivates and goes dry and salivates again; there is sweating and swelling and blackest depression; and the victim finally recovers after several days spent truly unpleasantly. There is no first-aid treatment for such a bite, although an antivenin is available.

Another inquiline with punch is the recluse or "violin" spider, *Loxosceles reclusa,* which inhabits the spaces between walls and furniture and other secluded and tranquil places. This species builds irregular webs similar to those of house spiders, in which other small inquilines are snared. In North America, recluse spiders nearly always bear a violin-shaped mark on the dorsal surface of the cephalothorax, the forward segment of the two segments of the body. The bite of the recluse is not as systemically virulent as that of the widow, but its venom does kill tissue around the bite, which then becomes more than ordinarily susceptible to infection. About a day after receiving a recluse bite, the patient experiences nausea, depression, and a horrible sequence of chills and fever, which may last up to three days. The flesh around the bite literally rots if it is not treated. An occasional victim suffers damage to the liver and kidneys as a result of the venom's action in breaking down red blood corpuscles, but most humans recover completely. The author, while visiting Texas, once put his foot into a shoe into which a specimen of *L. reclusa* had crawled during the night. The inquiline interloper bit the shoe's rightful owner on the instep, making him good and sick and forever scarring his scientific impartiality by instilling a lingering distaste for members of genus *Loxosceles*.

7 Almost Inquilines

When the European culture first began moving to the New World in a big way, it encountered native cultures which had carried on for many centuries a more or less unobtrusive ecological role. These cultures had long ago reached an equilibrium state with regard to the native American fauna, and there was in the fifteenth century little wide-spread ecological change occurring on the American landmasses. However, the European colonists changed all this with their intense exploitation of natural resources and consequent alteration of the landscape. Within a biological moment—about five hundred years—the entire ecological structure of the New World has been altered, and its elements, human and otherwise, are still experiencing the reverberations of that traumatic moment.

Within this ecological flux we find a few native species that are adaptable enough to be undergoing a transition from independent niches in the native ecology to inquilinistic niches in the European one. The problems faced by these animals in confronting the European invasion were totally different from those faced by the Eurasian inquilines that have coevolved with various civilizations since preagricultural times. The intricate and powerful European technology sprang upon the Americas full-blown, as it were, from the other side of the earth, equipped with firearms and all the other complex apparatus of sixteenth-century civiliza-

179

tion. Almost all the native mammals, including the humans, fell back before the efficiency of Europe. To this day, relatively few large or medium-sized native American mammals can be found outside the reservations that are variously called zoos, parks, and wildernesses.

As always, however, some animals have begun to prosper from the change. Although certain Eurasian birds and mammals had already saturated many ancient niches in the advancing civilization, new niches opened as the culture underwent the spectacular transition from agricultural to industrial economy. Human living habits, particularly in North America, have been drastically altered by the appearance of such rapid vehicles as trains and automobiles. The evolution of suburbs in particular has created a whole entourage of niches suitable to exploitation by mammals.

The proliferation of one-family homes surrounded by parcels of land in suburban industrial America resulted in the establishment of widespread medium-density human populations in artificially regulated local ecological communities. Large predators, excepting domesticated ones and humans themselves, are absent in such regulated communities, and the artificial influx of foodstuffs to feed the resident humans is great enough to allow an overflow supporting some fairly large mammals.

Back in the chapter on mice we encountered a Mesozoic relic, the opossum, *Didelphis marsupialis*. This uncomely beast, ratlike enough in appearance to have been responsible for many stories of "rats as big as cats," is the only marsupial native to what is now called the continental United States. At the coming of the European settlers the northern limit of the opossum's range, which extends south to Brazil, was the land adjoining the Gulf Coast and the southern Mississippi valley. However, the elimination of more competent mammals throughout much of the United States has permitted the rapid expansion of the opossum's range in the last century. Opossums now inhabit farmland and suburban areas north to New Hampshire and west to the Rockies. In addition they have been introduced in several places along the West Coast, where they thrive.

Opossums are omnivores. They have maintained themselves unchanged for eighty million years through having early perfected their knack of eating anything organic. Although they are rather slow, and certainly dull-witted for mammals, opossums make up for these traits by having two litters of up to fifteen young annually, extraordinary for such large mammals. At birth, the entire litter may fit ino a teaspoon, each young being a tiny, partially formed creature of but 2 grams' mass. These mites crawl into the pouch of their mother, where they affix themselves

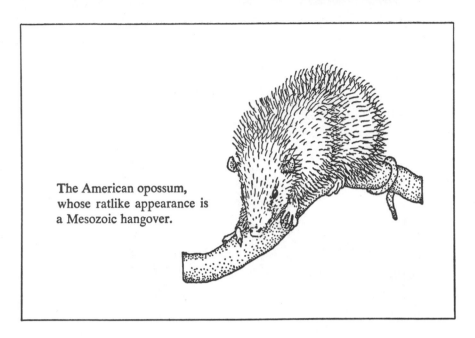

The American opossum, whose ratlike appearance is a Mesozoic hangover.

to one of up to seventeen nipples contained therein. Here they remain until they are furred and can see and get about, and to the pouch they return until they are too big, at about two months of age. Young opossums stay with the mother another two months or so, often hanging from her naked, prehensile tail with their own smaller versions of same.

Although the opossum is delicious eating and is considered a delicacy by many rural Americans, its uncouth appearance and slinking nocturnal ways place it at a low level in the dietary esteem of many suburbanites. Consequently in suburbs the opossum is safe in moving from garbage to orchard to garden in the night, when the dogs are locked up. Recalling that our ancestors were probably rather like opossums, we might regard their presence as an interesting confrontation with our humbler past. However, since the opossum is a garbage lover, a messy one at that, and often chooses to share our houses with us only to die in inaccessible corners of attics and the like, we tend to regard him as a nuisance at best. Opossums continue to do well, nonetheless, without the slightest regard for our tastes.

The squirrels of the genus *Sciurus* are familiar to nearly every suburban resident of the United States east of the Rockies. Originally residents of the vast forests of the continent, where they ate the seeds of trees, these rodents have in some cases flourished in the midst of mighty cities. Along the eastern seaboard the gray squirrel, *Sciurus carolinensis,* is the

Like most arboreal mammals, the gray squirrel is equipped with a large tail serving to steer the animal when it leaps through the air from branch to branch. In addition, the tail is flicked back and forth in the visual component of the "barking" display familiar to anyone who has ever treed a squirrel. Pictured here, the display is a threat gesture used in defense of territory.

most familiar form. Thriving in the heart of Manhattan as it never might in the remotest forests of Maine, the gray squirrel is friend to millions of city dwellers and suburbanites. In the larger towns and cities gray squirrels grow fat and bold on human charity much as do rock doves, but in suburban areas they are forced to seek food other than that handed to them in the park. Because the suburban ecology is so often closely regulated, such squirrels often come into conflict with their human landlords. Orchards and gardens may be subject to depredations by squirrels, as are birdfeeders and even garbage cans. Squirrels also occasionally steal eggs and young from bird nests. All in all, however, the grace conferred on suburbanites by the presence of these handsome squirrels far outweighs any trouble they may make.

Suburban gray squirrels are usually free from predation by any but dogs, cats, and humans. Cats and dogs make little impress on the squirrel population, but in some areas squirrels are actively hunted by humans armed with small-bore rifles and teamed with dogs. In such cases the squirrels respond by becoming wily and worthy prey, even against such formidable odds, and are thus highly esteemed as prey. They are delicious eating, too, and the autumn squirrel stew is a lordly gastronomic event. Across much of the continental United States the genus *Sciurus* is represented by the fox squirrel, *Sciurus niger*. Fox squirrels are larger than their gray cousins and occur in a number of colors, from tawny yellow to black. They inhabit open woods, towns, and small cities in the eastern United States from the Atlantic to the Rockies, and share throughout their range most of the habits of gray squirrels.

In the moister suburbs and small cities across North America a water-loving cousin of the bears and dogs is experiencing a population boom. The familiar raccoon, *Procyon lotor,* inhabits almost any place

His droll appearance belies the strength and temerity of the raccoon in a pinch. Mightily muscled and equipped with powerful teeth and claws, raccoons may kill dogs several times their own weight or tear steel traps or cages apart.

with enough water to form a small creek. As most human settlements occur in conjunction with water, the raccoons have experienced a good deal of selective pressure either to adapt to European civilization or to recede before it. The raccoon adapted, partly because it is an admirably generalized omnivorous carnivore of fairly primitive structure (note how often primitive structure has aided the chances of an inquiline mammal) and partly because its brain is so large and capable and its hands so agile, almost manlike. The raccoon has all the potential, it would seem, for the evolution of a technological descendant in the manner of man, should the latter species goof and become extinct.

Humans have long respected the cleverness of raccoons, and the animals consequently occupy a high level in the public esteem. This esteem unfortunately sometimes results in the capture of young raccoons for pets. While they are young the animals are playful and amusing, but mature raccoons are powerful and behaviorally unpredictable. Your author has been badly bitten by such a tame (i.e., unafraid-of-humans) raccoon and regards all such unhappy specimens as candidates for roasting. In many rural parts of the United States the sport of raccoon hunting is an important pursuit of many male adult humans equipped with specially bred and trained 'coonhounds. In suburban areas, where the discharge of firearms is so often censured, there is almost no predation on raccoons. The animals can easily deter most dogs and are considerably larger than cats, so that they raise their litters of four or so young with nearly a hundred percent success in many settled areas. Young raccoons remain with their mothers for about six months, learning the many tricks of the raccoon trade. Frequenting rivers and streamsides as they do, raccoons once ate many fish and crayfish and frogs, alternating these with nuts, and with berries and other succulent vegetation. Unlike those of many other carnivores, the teeth of raccoons are designed to grind vegetable food efficiently, and raccoons are frequent visitors to fields of maize and vegetable gardens. Where these are not available the animals turn to garbage, which is nearly always available. A good Westchester County raccoon can circumvent almost any protection the irate suburbanite cares to devise for his trash, and such a raccoon seems sometimes to spread trash about for amusement's sake alone.

Raccoons are members of the interesting carnivore family Procyonidae, which includes the pandas of Asia and the ringtails and coatis of the American tropics. Evolutionarily situated near the trunk of the tree from which sprang the dogs and bears (*procyon*, "before-dog"), the procyonids seem to have evolved in North America some twenty million

Long renowned for his voice and his cleverness, the coyote figures prominently in the mythology of many western North American aborigines. In Indian tales he occupies the position of Trickster, much in the manner of the Asian monkey-god Hanuman.

years ago. Although most procyonids are not faring well at the hands of humanity, the raccoon is flourishing throughout a range that extends from Hudson's Bay to Panama.

Probably descended from some raccoonlike ancestor are the dogs of genus *Canis,* of which our own *C. familiaris* is probably the most familiar example. Several species in this genus may cross with one another, producing fertile offspring; most notable of those able to pair across species are the domestic dog, the wolf (*C. lupus*), and the coyote or prairie wolf (*C. latrans*). In the wild the coyote is a distinctive lightly built wolflike dog whose lovely nocturnal calls have earned it the scientific name *C. latrans,* which means "barking dog." Formerly confined to open grassland where rabbits and rodents were plentiful food, the coyote has benefited by the near-extinction of its cousin the wolf and has appropriated most of the former range of the larger species. There are probably more coyotes alive now than in any other time, for the activities of

European civilization have provided these little wolves with a heaven on earth.

Although primarily carnivorous when prey is available, coyotes also feed on vegetation, including maize and garden crops. Berries and nuts are also favored and when in season may attract considerable numbers of coyotes. Hungry coyotes often eat the dung of large herbivores such as horses, and spend much time scavenging at dumps. Hunting coyotes tend to work alone or in pairs, unlike their pack-hunting relatives the wolves and domestic dogs. Thus they are usually limited to prey their own size or smaller, a strong alibi against the accusations of ranchers and sheepmen, who sometimes accuse the little dogs of pulling down animals the size of grown cattle. The very largest coyotes rarely exceed a mass of 23 kilograms, about 50 pounds, and most weigh considerably less. Much of the damage to livestock attributed to coyotes is actually the work of feral domestic dogs, which, larger than coyotes and running in packs, are able to do a great deal more harm. Still, coyotes take their toll in lambing time, and ewes and their offspring cut off from the flock in sudden blizzards are sometimes taken by coyotes. They are also occasional nocturnal visitors to henhouses. More often, however, coyotes find the carcasses of domestic stock dead from other causes. Being avid scavengers, they dig in to such finds in numbers, making the carcasses a favored place in which to set coyote traps.

After a gestation period of about sixty-two days, five to ten coyote puppies are born between March and April or May. The puppies open their eyes at twelve days, but they remain in the den until late June. During the rest of the summer, and sometimes through the following autumn and into the winter, the young pups accompany their mother on her rounds, learning and sometimes assisting in the chase. The pups reach full size in the fall, when they are often trapped for their fur.

Although they were mainly animals of the West before the European invasion, coyotes have since extended their range east to New Hampshire, spanning the continent. Their northern limit is the north coast of Alaska and their southern limit is Panama, making them one of the most widespread of North American mammals. In suburbs they abandon hunting for dump-scavenging and occasional pet-stealing; suburbanites of Los Angeles sometimes complain of having had kittens nabbed by coyotes. In some towns crosses between domestic dogs and coyotes are common, in isolated settlements sometimes producing localized canine breeds of striking handsomeness. It is possible that, as the coyote associates increasingly with human beings, its genetic structure will become more and more indistinguishable from that of the domestic dog, although this process is not yet widespread.

Coyotes are wily creatures by nature, and the constant warfare waged by stockmen against them has produced great numbers of very smart coyotes, sternly selected through centuries of being trapped and hunted with the best weaponry that European technology had to offer. The commonest implement brought to bear against coyotes is the steel trap, cunningly hidden and attractively baited. Entire volumes have been written on methods of trapping the coyote, but the little rascal continues to increase in both numbers and range. This is perhaps to our benefit in the end, for coyotes are undoubtedly among the most prepossessing of our inquilines.

In cities and other habitations of humans, the fundamental input of food energy is through grains and other domesticated plants imported to these partly sterile places by human agency. The idea behind the entire system of food transportation and storage is to remove biomass from the general system and trap it in the artificial system so that its location and use at any point is under human management and is directed toward enlarging the artificial system. The living system at large, always gravitating toward the stability of a multiform ecosystem, is confronted with the problem of overcoming human ingenuity and creating diversity amidst the desolation of our works.

For the past twenty or thirty thousand years the number of mammalian and avian species has declined markedly, first in conjunction with the initial spread of humanity and, later, with the bloom of the technologically advanced European culture. As the twentieth century draws to a close we begin to see the final mopping-up of biomass by the artificial system. The last great herds of herbivorous mammals, in the taiga of the north and the savannas of Africa, are faced with the relentless pressure of growing human numbers around them. The last sizable vertebrate predators, the lions, wolves, eagles, and hawks, are driven to the brink of extinction. It begins to seem as if the collective goal of humanity is that the world be populated only by humans and their food plants and animals.

However, in the face of this mopping-up process we are reminded of the tremendous elasticity of the living system, its ability to restore complexity and stability despite determined human efforts toward unstable simplicity. Life springs back with a thousand strange and beautiful beings designed to utilize the wastes of the city, the monocultured deserts of wheat, rice, and maize. In any part of the planet on which humans live, their lives are to some extent dedicated to the support of a legion of inquilines, some of which we never even see as we feed them. Life responds to our efforts by filling every chink, every minuscule gap in our food system with a little animal perfectly designed to profit from our errors.

Index

Acarina, 170–71
Achaearanea, 171
Acheta domesticus, 157
Agelenidae, 172
Albatross, 99, 101
Algae, 5, 7
Allosaur, 30
Alphitobius diaperinus, 161
Amblypygi, 168
American Acclimatization Society, 62
American Racing Pigeon Association, 84
Anaerobism, 5
Angoumois, 158
Anobiidae, 162
Antibiotics, 128
Antrodemus, 30
Ants, 15, 164–65
Aphids, 16, 169
Arachnida, 166–71
Aranea, 171
Archaeopteryx, 32, 33, 99
Archosauria, 35
Archosaurians, 108, 109
Aristotle, 121
Army Signal Corps, U.S., homing
  pigeons and, 84
Arthropoda, ix
Arthropods, 151–75
Aspergillosis, 89
Aspergillus fumigatus, 89
Autotomy, 170
Autotrophs, 6, 8
Aztecs, 130–31

Bacteria, 5, 90
Bandicota bengalensis, 134, 135
Barbary doves, 79
Barley, 26
Barnacles, 153
Batrachomyomachy, 121
Bats, 33, 94, 106, 110, 111, 170
Beavers, 113
Bedbugs, 169
Bees, 15, 164
Beetles, ix, 158–62
  carpet, 169
  cigarette, 162
  "darkling," 160
  deathwatch, 162
  drugstore, 162

flour, 160–61
fungus, 162–63
grain, 160
granary, 160
Japanese, 73
larder, 159–60
rove, 14, 15
"snout," 162
spider, 161
Biomasses, 16, 17, 31, 187
Biomes, 17
Birds, 7, 21–102, 116, 170, 180
  respiratory system, 94–95
  See also under names of birds
Black Death, 127
Black widow spider, 173–74
Blackbirds, 48, 59, 71
Blatella germanica, 156
Blatta orientalis, 156
Blattidae, 155
Bluebirds, 29, 52
Book lice, 157, 158
"Book scorpion." *See* Pseudoscorpions
Bostrichidae, 161
Bristletails, 14
Brooklyn Institute, 28
Bubonic plague, 127
Butterflies, 158

Calvaria major, 80–81
Candida albicans, 90
Canis, 185
Canis latrans. See Coyotes
Canis lupus. See Wolves
Capybara, 107, 112
Caribou, 9
Carpet beetle, 169
Caterpillars, 158
Cats, house, 120, 126, 127, 133, 145,
  183
Cattle, 11, 26
Caviomorpha, 112
Cavy, 112
Cellulose, 14
Centipedes, 152, 153, 154
Centruroides, 167
Cercaria, 92
Chaetopterus, 12
Cheese mites, 170
Chelicerata, 166

Chelifer cancroides, 169
Chiggers, 91
Chilopods, 153
Chiracanthium, 172
Chiroptera, 111
Chordata, 152
Cigarette beetle, 162
Cleaner, false, 8
Cleaner wrasse, 8
Cleridae, 160
Clothes moth, 158
Coatonachthodes, 15
Cockroaches, 14, 155–57, 172
    American, 156
    Australian, 156
    German, 156
    Oriental, 156
    tropical, 156
Coleoptera, 158
Collared doves, 79
Color patterns, 8
Columba livia. See Doves, rock
Columba oenas. See Doves, stock
Columbidae, 81
Columbiformes, 79–80, 81, 91, 93
Commensalism, 9, 10
Contagione, De (Fracastorius), 129
Corals, 13
Cowbirds, 7, 71
Coyotes, 185–87
Crabs, 12, 152, 153, 166
Crayfish, 153
Cricetidae, 113
Crickets, 155, 157
Crocodiles, 35
Crows, 46
Crustaceans, 7, 14, 152, 153
Cryptococcus neoformans, 89
Cuckoo, 7
Curculionidae, 162

Daddy longlegs. *See* Harvestmen
"Darkling beetles," 160
Deathwatch beetle, 162
Deer, 8–9, 14
Dermestes lardarius. See Larder beetle
Dermestidae, 159
Didelphis, 109, 180–81
Dimetrodon, 107–108, 117
Dinosaurs, 30–35
Diptera, 163–64
Dodos, 80–81, 91

Dogs, 127, 145, 181, 183, 184, 185,
    186
Domestication, 10, 16, 77, 78, 82, 85,
    86, 87
Dormice, 113
Doves
    Barbary, 79
    collared, 79
    Inca, 79
    rock, 77–102
        courtship, 87
        domestication, 77, 78, 82, 85, 86, 87
        nests, 87
    stock, 78
    turtle, 79
    white, 82, 86
    See also Pigeons
Dragonflies, 97
Drugstore beetle, 162

Eagles, 187
Earthworms, 152
Echidna, 109
Ecology, 18, 19
Economics, 18
Ecosystems, 16
Ectoparasites, 16
Ectopistes migratorius. See
    Pigeons, passenger
Ectotherms, 32
Eels, moray, 8
Encephalitis, 92
Endotherms, 31, 32
Ethology, 43
Eurypterids, 166
Eutherians, 109–10
Eyeworms, 92

Falconiformes, 93
Falcons, 68, 70, 73, 86, 93, 101
False cleaner, 8
Fannia canicularis, 163
Fannia scalaris, 164
Feathers, 32–39
Felis domesticus, 120
    See also Cats, house
Ferrets, 11–12, 145
Filter-feeders, 12
Finches, 24
Firebrat, 154, 155
Flatworms, 92
Fleas, 91, 105, 127–30

Flies, 14, 105, 153, 163–64
  black, 92
  false stable, 164
  hippoboscid, 92
  house, 163, 173–74
  latrine, 163, 164
  nocturnal, 173
  pigeon, 91
Flour beetle, 160–61
Flukes, 92
Fossils, 5
Fracastorius, 129
Fungi, 7, 16, 162–63
Fungus beetles, 162–63

Genghis Khan, homing pigeons and, 83, 84
Gerbils, 113, 144
Gophers, 113
Grackles, 71
Grain beetle, 160
Grain borer, lesser, 161
Granary beetle, 160
Grasses, 16, 17, 26
Grasshoppers, 155
Green algae, 7
"Grocer's itch," 170
Grouse, sand, 80
Guinea pigs, 112, 144
Gunflint Chert, 5

Ham beetle, 160
Hamsters, 113, 144
Harvestmen, 167, 169–70
Hawks, 73, 86, 105, 187
Herbst corpuscles, 38
Heterotrophs, 6, 8
Histoplasma capsulatum, 71, 89
Horseshoe crab, 152, 166
Houlton, Maine, 160–61
Hymenoptera, 164
Hystricomorpha, 113

Inca doves, 79
Inquilinism, 4, 10, 11, 12
Insects, 152–75
  flight, 96–97
Isopods, 92, 153
Japanese beetle, 73
Jays, 46
Jerboas, 113

Kangaroos, 110

Lactrodectus mactans, 173
Larder beetle, 159–60
Lasioderma serricorne, 162
Lepidoptera, 158
Lepinotus inquilinus, 157
Lepisma saccharina, 154
Lesser grain borer, 161
Lice, 72, 91, 92, 128–31
  book, 157, 158
Lichens, 7
Limulus, 152
Linnaeus, Carolus, 106
Lions, 187
Living Mammals of the World (Sanderson), 125
Lizards, 31, 35, 43
Lobsters, 153
Loxosceles reclusa, 174–75

Malaria, 92
Mammals, 105–11, 116, 128, 137, 139, 170, 180
Mandibulata, 152
Mantids, 155
Mao Tse-tung, homing pigeons and, 84
Mars, 7
Marsupials, 109, 110
Martins, 29
Masseter muscle, 111–12
Meal moths, 158
Mealworms, 161
Metacercaria, 92
Metatherians, 109–10
Mice, 103–34
  deer, 43, 113
  grasshopper, 113
  harvest, 113
  house, 106, 111, 114–22, 126, 127, 134
  jumping, 113
  North American, 113
  Old World, 113
  pygmy, 106
Microbes, 14
Milk, pigeon's, 81, 87–88
Millipedes, 14, 152
Miracidium, 92
Mistletoe, 7
Mites, 14, 72, 91, 167, 170
Moles, 111

Moniliasis, 90
Monkeys, 170
   See also Primates
Monomorium pharaonis, 164
Moray eels, 8
Mosquitoes, 92
Moths, 158
"Mountain beaver." See Sewellel
Mouse. See Mice
Muridae, 106, 113–16
Murinae, 114
Muroidae, 113
Mus musculus. See Mice, house
Musca domesticus, 163
Muscidae, 163
Muscina stabulans, 164
Mustela nigripes, 11
Mutualism, 7–8, 10, 14, 16, 17, 77, 78,
   110
Mynas, 58
Myomorpha, 113
Myriapods, 152, 153

Necrobia rufipes, 160
Newcastle disease, 90
Nicotiana, 162

Oniscoidea, 153
Opossums, 109, 110, 180
Ornithosis, 90
Orthoptera, 155
Oryzaephilus surinamensis, 160
Oscines, 23–24, 57
Ostomidae, 160
Owls, 11, 12, 73, 105

Paramys, 111
Parasites, 6–7, 8, 16, 29, 89–91, 116,
   128–29, 130, 133, 153, 170–71
   pigeons and, 89–92
   starlings and, 71–72
Parasitism, 6, 10
Parrots, 46, 70, 81, 90
Passer domesticus. See Sparrows, house
Passer montanus. See Sparrows, tree
Passeriformes, 25, 51, 57
Pasteurella pestis, 127–28
Pauropods, 153
Peanuts, 7
Pear trees, 7–8
Pecten, 40–41
Pediculus humanus, 128

Pelycosaurs, 107–108
Periplaneta americana, 156
Periplaneta australasiae, 156
Phalangida, 169
Pharaoh ants, 164–65
Photosynthesis, 5
Pigeon pox, 92
Pigeons, 75–102, 170
   bacterial infections and, 90
   breeding, 82, 83, 85, 86
   Carrier, 83, 84
   circulatory system, 95–96
   diet, 88
   flight, 96–102
   fungal diseases and, 89–90
   homing, 82, 83–86
   parasites and, 89–92
   passenger, 91
   racing, 83, 84
   religious significance, 82, 83
   respiratory system, 94–95
   virus diseases and, 90
   See also Doves
Pigeon's milk, 81, 87–88
Pigs, 7
Pike, Nicholas, 28
Pill bugs, 92, 153
Placenta, 109, 110
Placentals, 109–11
Plague, 127–28, 133
Platypus, 109
Plautus, 121
Pliny the Elder, 121
Ploceidae, 24
Popillia japonica. See Japanese beetle
Porcupines, 112–13
Prairie dogs, 11–12
Prairie wolf. See Coyotes
Predation, 8
Primates, 111
   See also Monkeys
Procyon lotor. See Raccoons
Procyonids, 183–85
Pseudoscorpions, x, 15, 167, 168, 169
Psittaciformes, 81
Psittacosis, 90
Psocoptera, 157–58
Psyllipsocidae, 157
Pteranodon, 101
Pteroclididae, 80
Pterosaurs, 32–35, 98–99, 101
Ptinidae, 161
Pyralis, 158

Rabbits, 127
Raccoons, 183–85
Racing, pigeon, 83, 84
Ramses III, Pharaoh, homing pigeons and, 82
Raphidae, 80
Raphus cucullus. See Dodos
Rats, 106, 113, 123–47
  Alexandrian. *See Rattus rattus*
  as human food, 144–45
  Bengal. *See Bandicota bengalensis*
  black. *See Rattus rattus*
  brown. *See Rattus norvegicus*
  burrowing, 113, 142
  cane, 113
  domesticated, 143, 144
  elimination of, 145
  fruit. *See Rattus rattus*
  gray. *See Rattus norvegicus*
  "house," 119, 131
  kangaroo, 113
  North American, 113
  Norway. *See Rattus norvegicus*
  Old World, 113
  rock, 113
  roof. *See Rattus rattus*
  sewer. *See Rattus norvegicus*
  water. *See Rattus norvegicus*
  wharf. *See Rattus norvegicus*
  wood, 113
Rattus, 125
Rattus exulans, 134, 135
Rattus norvegicus (wanderratte), 111, 125, 131–34, 138–40, 144
Rattus rattus, 125–31, 133, 134, 138, 139, 140
Recluse ("violin") spider, 174–75
Reptiles, 31, 107–108, 116
  See also Crocodiles; Snakes
Respiration, 5
Rhyzopertha dominica, 161
Rickettsiae, 128–30
Roaches. *See* Cockroaches
Robins, 51, 71
Rock doves. *See* Doves, rock; Pigeons
Rodents, 105–47
  See also Mice; Rats; Squirrels
Rove beetle, 14, 15

Salmonellae, 90
Sand grouse, 80
Sanderson, Ivan T., 125
Sandstone, 7

Sarcoptiformes, 170
Scardafella inca. See Doves, Inca
Scheifflin, Eugene, 62
Sciuromorpha, 112
Sciurus. See Squirrels
Scorpions, 165, 166, 167–69
Scutigera, 153
Scutigerella, 154
Secale, 17
Sewellel, 112
Shakespeare, William, 62
Shrews, 111
Shrikes, 57
Shrimp, 153
Silverfish, 154
Sitophilus granarius, 162
Sitophilus oryzae, 162
Sitotroga, 158
Smoky Girl (prize-winning pigeon), 84
Snails, 92
Snakes, 11, 34, 105
"Snout beetles," 162
Sow bugs, 92, 153
Sparrows
  "English," 27
  grassland, 26
  house, 21–54, 57, 61, 62
    brain, 42–46
    circadian rhythm, 47–48
    classification, 23
    distribution, 27
    evolution, 29–31
    eyes, 39–41
    feathers, 31–39
    flocks, 48
    gonads, 49–50
    nests, 52
    reproductive behavior, 50–52
    subspecies, 27
  tree, 26, 27
Spider beetles, 161
Spiders, x, 14, 166, 167, 171–75
  black widow, 173–74
  house, 171–72
    European, 172
  recluse ("violin"), 174–75
  sac, 172
Spriggina, 152
Springtails, 14
Squabs, 79, 83, 87–88
  See also Pigeons
Squeakers, 87–88
Squirrels, 112, 131, 181–83

Squirrels (*cont.*)
　arboreal, 112
　bald-tailed, 131
　fox, 183
　gray, 181–83
　ground, 112
Staphylinidae, ix
Starlings, 24, 48, 55–74
　airport problem, 72
　as human food, 73–74
　as pets, 74
　beneficial tasks of, 73
　classification, 57
　common, 57–74
　digestive systems, 63–66
　eradication attempts, 73
　eyesight, 62
　flocks, 67–68
　food consumption, 6–67
　hearing, 70
　language, 67–69
　migration, 59–60
　parasites and, 71–72
　range of, 61–62
　roosts, 70–71
　rose, 61
　threat stance of, 68
　water consumption, 67
Stegobium paniceum, 162
Stock doves, 78
Stoneflies, 97
Strabo, 121
Streptococci, 90
Streptopelia decaoto. See Doves,
　collared
Streptopelia risoria. See Doves, Barbary
Streptopelia turtur. See Turtledoves
Sturnidae, 57
Sturnus rosea. See Starlings, rose
Sturnus vulgaris. See Starlings, common
Supella supellectilium, 156
Swallows, 29
Symbiosis, x, 4, 6, 7, 8, 10, 11, 16, 26, 77,
　89, 92, 128
Symphylans, 153–54
Synapsids, 107
Syrinx, 69, 95

Taenia, 6
Taeniolabis, 109
Tapeworms, 6, 92
Tegenaria, 172
Tenebrio molitor, 161

Tenebrionidae, 160
Tenebroides mauritanicus, 160
Termitaries, 14–15
Termites, 14–15, 16
Testosterone, 115
Tetracycline, 128
Thecodonts, 108
Therapsids, 108, 109
Theridion, 171
Thermobia domestica, 154
Thomas à Becket, 130
Thrush, 90
Thysanura, 154
Thysanuran, 15
Ticks, 72, 91, 92, 167
Tineola biselliella, 158
Titmice, 48
Tribolium confusum, 160
Triggerfish, 13
Trilobites, 152, 166
Trogium pulsatorium, 157
Truculentus (Plautus), 121
Turtledoves, 79
Tutankhamen, tomb of, 162
Typhus, 128–31, 133
Tyrannosaurus, 35

United States Agency for International
　Development, 144
Uropygi, 169

Vaccum activity, 58
Vertebrates, 151
"Violin" spider, 174–75
Voles, 113

Wanderratte. *See Rattus norvegicus*
"War of Frogs and Mice," 121
Washington, George, 130
Wasps, 164
"Water bug," 156
Weasels, 11–12
Weavers, 24–26, 29, 51
Weevils, 162
Wheat, 26, 188
Wolves, 8–9, 10, 185, 186, 187
　prairie, 185–87
Worms, 7, 12, 92, 152, 163
　See also Earthworms; Eyeworms;
　　Flatworms; Mealworms; Tape-
　　worms
Wrasse, cleaner, 8
Wrens, house, 52